FRIENDSHIP BLOCKS

NEW SETTINGS FOR SENTIMENTAL FAVORITES

Marge Edie

Martingale™
& COMPANY

Friendship Blocks:
New Settings for Sentimental Favorites
© 2001 by Marge Edie

& C O M P A N Y

That Patchwork Place® is an imprint
of Martingale & Company.

Martingale & Company
20205 144th Ave. NE
Woodinville, WA 98072-8478
www.martingale-pub.com

Printed in Hong Kong
06 05 04 03 02 01   8 7 6 5 4 3 2 1

- Credits -
President: Nancy J. Martin
CEO: Daniel J. Martin
Publisher: Jane Hamada
Editorial Director: Mary V. Green
Managing Editor: Tina Cook
Technical Editor: Darra Williamson
Copy Editor: Liz McGehee
Design and Production Manager: Stan Green
Illustrator: Laurel Strand
Cover and Text Designer: Regina Girard
Photographer: Brent Kane

Library of Congress Cataloging-in-Publication Data
Edie, Marge.
    Friendship blocks : new settings for sentimental
    favorites / Marge Edie.
        p. cm.
    ISBN 1-56477-385-X
    1. Quilting—Patterns. 2. Patchwork—Patterns.
    3. Friendship quilts. I. Title.
TT835 .E376 2001
746.46'041—dc21   2001044557

Mission Statement
We are dedicated to providing quality products and
service by working together to inspire creativity
and to enrich the lives we touch.

On the title page: "When Friendship Blooms" by Catherine
M. Dyer, 2000, Simpsonville, South Carolina, 90" x 90". The
time Cathy spent at her design wall, planning and dreaming,
nearly equals the time she spent executing the piecing and
extensive appliqué in this masterpiece. The story of her
creation is almost as wonderful as the finished product, which
won best of show at the Nimble Thimbles Quilt Guild
exhibit. She referenced Barbara Brackman's *Encyclopedia of
Pieced Quilt Patterns* (American Quilters Society, 1993) and
Judy Hopkins's *Around the Block* (Martingale & Company,
2000) for her piecing plan. Her floral appliqué work came
from the patterns in *Grandmother's Garden Quilt* by Eleanor
Burns and Patricia Knoechel (Quilt in a Day, 2001) and from
Fabled Flowers by Kumiko Sudo (McGraw Hill, 1996).

Contents

Circle of Friends *by Kay Kirk, 2000, Fountain Inn, South Carolina, 90" x 104";*
machine quilted by Jennifer Kay. Using her Rail Fence exchange blocks in a Storm
at Sea setting allowed Kay to develop quite a large quilt. She used floral fabrics as
a lovely complement to the signature blocks she received.

Preface

Is there an Ohio University art major from the 1960s who doesn't remember Charles Smith? He taught many of my required courses, but I think of him as my "lettering" professor. Back before computer-generated calligraphy, it was necessary to learn to do it all by hand with the aid of India ink, special pen tips, and steady concentration. I loved it so much that I wanted that for my profession. Nothing sounded better to me than working up the verses inside American Greetings or Hallmark cards.

Art majors study drawing and design. Semesters of figure drawing, watercolor, and life sculpture pointed out that I was not terribly good at drawing. It was a hard but necessary lesson. Closer to graduation, I took weaving and learned what I could be passionate about: fiber, geometry, and design.

Life led me in other directions, but now it has brought me full circle, back to one of my early art interests. Math, mechanical design structures, and symmetry spark my imagination. So here it is, all wrapped up in one neat package. And thank you, Dr. Smith, for your perseverance in the classroom.

Introduction

Just when you think that you've seen—and maybe quilted—it all, something happens to trigger a new creative binge. That's what happened to me when Ann Hawkins and other board members challenged our Lake and Mountain Quilters to a millennium signature block exchange, using two very traditional and simple block structures: Rail Fence and a Nine Patch variation.

This guild means a lot to me, and its members include many of my very best friends, so I decided to be a sport and partake. However, the idea of a lot of Rail Fence and Nine Patch Variation blocks in a standard setting did not spark my interest at all. So I decided to try some alternatives on the computer. I was thrilled with the many configurations that emerged and returned to our next meeting with various suggestions for any members who might also be looking for something a little different. A few of my friends elected to try some of my ideas, and others went ahead with their own wonderful visions. At the autumn 1999 deadline, we were all delighted to see such beautiful quilts!

Several of the projects in this book are the result of this initial challenge, and others of a similar challenge by the Nimble Thimbles Quilt Guild in Mauldin, South Carolina, so you will see many repeat signatures. Other projects make use of two additional interchangeable blocks: the Snowball and Diagonal Strip blocks.

Combined with interesting sashing, these few simple blocks lead to some really exciting geometries. In this book you will learn how to make the basic signature blocks, do attractive and interesting lettering, design and construct dynamic sashing, complete the piece with either hand or machine quilting, and make binding in a width of your choice.

The projects make wonderful commemorative or tribute quilts. Every band director, retiring teacher, or den mother would treasure a quilted piece featuring the names of people who were important for a special time in his or her life. Clubs love to display these hangings at meetings, and having guests sign individual squares is a perfect way to commemorate a wedding. I hope you are inspired by the possibilities!

The Basics

Equipment and Supplies

Sewing Supplies

You will need a reliable straight-stitch sewing machine to construct the quilt tops in this book. Use a size 70/10 or 80/12 sewing machine needle, and replace it frequently as needed. Set your machine to sew about ten stitches per inch, or a little less than the number 2 on foreign machines.

Precision piecing will, as always, result in the best quilt tops. If your sewing machine accepts a quarter-inch foot, attach it and use it for piecing.

Use a good-quality 100 percent–cotton or cotton-covered polyester thread in your machine and in the bobbin. Pick a color to blend with your fabric selection. Gray or some other neutral is often a good choice.

You will also need fabric shears, pins, a seam ripper, quilting needles, quilting thread, an iron and ironing board or surface, and a plastic spray bottle filled with water to dampen your fabric before pressing.

Rotary-Cutting Supplies

Pick your favorite brand of rotary mat, cutter, and acrylic quilter's ruler. The larger mats are handiest for cutting multiple thicknesses and larger pieces of fabric, while the smaller ones are useful when cutting strips from your scrap collection. Store the cutting mat away from heat to prevent it from warping.

Choose a 6" x 24" ruler, with easy-to-read ⅛" markings. Replace it if the cutting edge gets nicked.

You'll also need a Bias Square® ruler, which was designed by Nancy J. Martin and is used for creating half-square-triangle units from bias strips.

Pens

For lettering, select only those pens designed for permanent adherence to fabric. If you purchase them from suppliers such as a quilt shop or favorite quilt catalog, you can be pretty sure that they are appropriate for your use. However, if you find permanent-ink pens at art-supply houses, test the pens for color durability, and make sure they don't come with a warning about harming fabrics.

Use each pen to write on a scrap of the desired fabric. Heat-set the ink with an iron, and then see what happens if you wet the material. If the color runs, do not use that particular pen. Make sure you test all the pens you plan to use. One color might be acceptable and another might not, even though it is made by the same manufacturer.

I rely heavily on Pigma pens, which are available in a rainbow of hues, but have made use of many other brands on various projects. Conduct your own "consumer testing" before you move ahead, and you will be happiest with the end results.

Other Supplies

Freezer paper makes a great stabilizer as you transfer your signature or lettering to fabric. Some of my friends use interesting fonts on their computers to print out names or other phrases and then trace these images onto the fabric, so a light box can be a valuable tool also.

I frequently use a mechanical pencil to make really fine lines on the signature fabric. A ruler is helpful for some people (like me) who need help keeping their lettering horizontal. I often draw a baseline to act as a guide for the lettering, then sketch the letters very faintly. Again, practice on test fabric to make sure that you aren't writing too heavily and that you are able to erase the marks if desired. A kneadable or soap eraser is great for removing lead without abrading the fabric.

If you wish to design your own quilting patterns, use template plastic and a utility knife to cut the design. There are many markers available in quilt specialty shops or from mail-order catalogs for tracing the pattern onto your fabric.

Fabrics

There are varying approaches to the projects in this book. With one option, participating quilters select their own fabrics, then prepare and exchange the basic blocks that make up the project. In this case, you will have a color surprise when you receive the blocks, and you may then decide on one—or many—fabric(s) for the sashing, borders, and binding.

Another way to make a signature quilt is to personally select perhaps four or five compatible fabrics, construct the blocks yourself, and have your friends sign them. Most likely, your sashing, border, and binding fabrics will be chosen from these same fabrics; or you may decide to go totally scrappy and let value and harmony dictate the selection of a large color palette from your stash. The instructions for each project in this book suggest a specific approach, depending on the design and size of the finished quilt, but you may alter any plan and make your own choice between yardage and scraps.

Use plain or subtly colored fabric for the signature area. Don't be afraid of delicate tone-on-tone prints as long as any surface printing doesn't repel the ink and keep it from settling into the fabric. Keep in mind that all 100 percent–cotton quilting fabric is not created equal. Before committing to any fabric for the signature portion of your blocks, test your pens to make sure the ink will not "travel" through the individual fibers to another part of the block. Tightly woven fabrics help retain the clarity of the lettering, but a sharp image also depends on the fibers not absorbing the ink as though the color were shooting out like sparklers!

Some of the best signature quilts are made from scraps. If you prefer this approach, sort your scraps by value. Select the palest, with the least amount of contrast, for the signature strips or squares; then decide if the sashing or the remaining pieces of the signature blocks will utilize the medium tones or darkest hues. The quilt's overall geometry will be best highlighted if you remain somewhat consistent with the arrangement of values. At the same time, this approach will allow you to incorporate a wide range of colors.

If your guild or group does a block exchange where the choice of fabric is left to each quilter, be sure to set guidelines. For our guild's millennium challenge, the "rule of thumb" was to select midtone, pretty prints and to avoid spotty designs. In my project "A Moment of My Time," at right, you might find some variations on that instruction, but the overall effect is very pleasing. To tie the quilt together, I selected a variety of similar prints for the triangular wedges and sashing. To me, the neutral greens seemed to blend well with the group of signature blocks I had received in the exchange. As you look through the book, however, you will notice other quilts from that same challenge and block exchange that have totally different results. One unifying feature is that we all started with the same muslin.

Wash and iron your fabrics to remove any surface finish which could, in time, react with the ink in your pens and possibly cause the fabric to deteriorate. Wash large pieces in the washing machine and smaller pieces by hand. If the rinse water shows color bleeding from the fabric, wash and rinse the fabric again. If the color still bleeds, discard the fabric as unsuitable for quilting. Dry your fabric in the clothes dryer, and press.

A Moment of My Time by Marge Edie, 1999, Clemson, South Carolina, 36" x 57".

Rotary Cutting

The cutting directions for all strips and pieces in this book include ¼"-wide seam allowances. Practice with the rotary equipment on fabric scraps if you are unfamiliar with these tools. Remember that the rotary blade is very sharp; be sure to slip the safety guard back into place after each cut you make.

1. Fold the fabric, selvages together and right sides out, aligning the crosswise and lengthwise grains as much as possible.

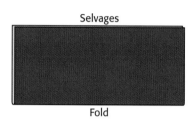

Selvages

Fold

If desired, fold the fabric a second time to create four thicknesses. Place the fabric on the cutting mat, with the folded edge parallel to the horizontal lines on the mat.

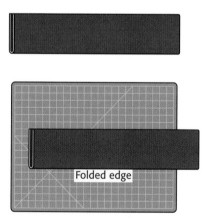

Folded edge

2. Place the edge of your ruler parallel to the vertical lines on the mat, and trim away the uneven end of the folded fabric. If you are right-handed, trim the left edge of the fabric; reverse if you are left-handed. Pressing down firmly with the ruler hand, cut off the ragged edges, pushing the rotary cutter away from yourself. Be sure to cut through all the layers of fabric.

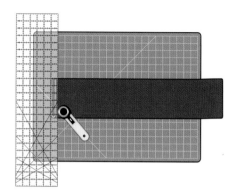

3. To cut strips, use your quilter's ruler to measure the desired width from the fabric's newly cut edge. Cut the desired number of strips, making sure to cut through all fabric layers.

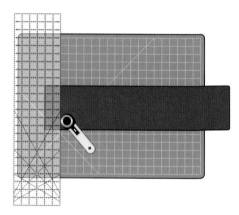

4. To cut squares or rectangles, cut a strip of fabric the required width. Trim off the selvage ends of the strip and place it on the mat, parallel with the horizontal lines on the mat. Measure as before and cut the required number of pieces, always cutting away from yourself.

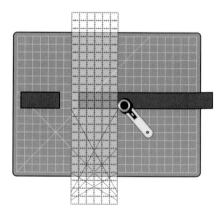

Sewing

Consistent ¼" seams ensure that the blocks you construct finish to the expected size. Many sewing machines include a special presser foot that measures exactly ¼" from the center needle position to the edge of the foot. This allows you to guide fabric through the machine with a perfect ¼"-wide seam. If your machine doesn't have such a foot, create a seam guide by placing several layers of tape ¼" to the right of the needle, and align your fabric against that as you sew.

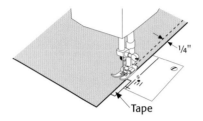

Pressing

Press each seam after stitching and before attaching other pieces. Begin by pressing the seam flat to smooth out any puckers.

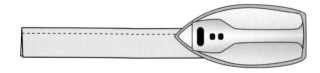

Then open the sewn pieces and, working from the right side of the fabric, press the seam toward the darker fabric. Use the iron to push the fabric over the seam. Be careful not to stretch the fabric as you press.

Occasionally, you will be instructed to press the seams open. In these instances, work from the wrong side of the fabric and press very carefully to avoid creases in the seam allowance.

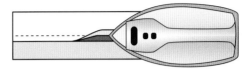

Pressing arrows are included in the project illustrations. Follow these arrows to ensure smooth construction of blocks and quilt tops.

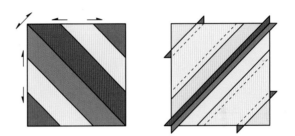

L&M Friendship Quilt by Fran Smink, 1999, Easley, South Carolina, 44" x 44". Elegant quilting complements simple blocks in this quilt. Fran first selected the twining quilt pattern and then designed her block arrangement to fit that plan and showcase her hand quilting. To read more about quilting, see pages 26–27.

Making the Signature Blocks

The quilts in this book are composed of four different signature blocks, which are arranged in a variety of ways. For practical purposes, all the blocks finish to 4½" square (5" unfinished).

Rail Fence Blocks

Method One

Use this method to make blocks from yardage. It yields 8 blocks, each finishing 4½" square (5" unfinished).

1. From muslin or other light signature fabric, cut 1 strip, 2" x 42". From print fabric, cut 2 strips, each 2" x 42". Print strips may be cut from the same fabric or from 2 different prints.
2. Sew the signature strip between the 2 print strips to make a strip set measuring 5" x 42". Press seams toward the print strips.
3. Crosscut the strip set into 8 Rail Fence blocks, each 5" square.

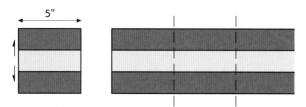

Method Two

Use this method to make blocks from scraps. It yields 1 block, finishing 4½" square (5" unfinished).

1. From muslin or other light signature fabric, cut 1 rectangle, 2" x 5". From print scraps, cut 2 rectangles, each 2" x 5". Print pieces may be cut from the same fabric or from 2 different prints.

2. Sew the signature rectangle between the 2 print rectangles. Press seams toward the print rectangles.

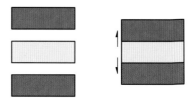

My Stitchin' Friends *by Jenny Grobusky, 2000, Walhalla, South Carolina, 70" x 88". In this bed-size quilt, Rail Fence and Nine Patch Variation exchange blocks shine brightly in the middle of beautiful blue stars. Simple alternate blocks balance the different colors used in the exchange blocks.*

Nine Patch Variation Blocks

Method One

Use this method to make blocks from yardage. It yields 10 blocks, each finishing 4½" square (5" unfinished).

1. From muslin or other light signature fabric, cut 1 strip, 2" x 42". From print fabric, cut 2 strips, each 2" x 42". Print strips may be cut from the same fabric or from 2 different prints.

2. Sew the signature strip between the 2 print strips to make a strip set measuring 5" x 42". Press seams toward the print strips.

3. Crosscut the strip set into 20 segments, each 2" x 5".

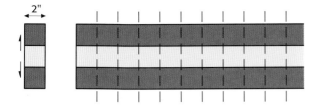

4. From the signature fabric, cut 1 strip, 5" x 42". Crosscut this strip into 10 rectangles, each 2" x 5".

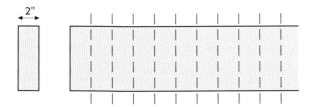

5. Sew a 2" x 5" signature rectangle between 2 pieced segments from step 3. Press seams toward the pieced segments. Make 10 blocks.

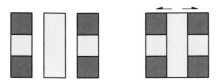

Method Two

Use this method to make blocks from scraps. It yields 1 block, finishing 4½" square (5" unfinished).

1. From muslin or other light signature fabric, cut 1 rectangle, 2" x 4". From print scraps, cut 2 rectangles, each 2" x 4". Print pieces may be cut from the same fabric or from 2 different prints.

2. Sew the signature rectangle between the 2 print rectangles to make a pieced unit that measures 4" x 5". Press seams toward the print rectangles.

3. Crosscut the unit into 2 segments, each 2" x 5".

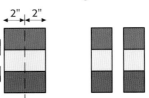

4. From the signature fabric, cut 1 rectangle, 2" x 5". Sew the 2" x 5" signature rectangle between the 2 pieced segments from step 3. Press seams toward the pieced segments.

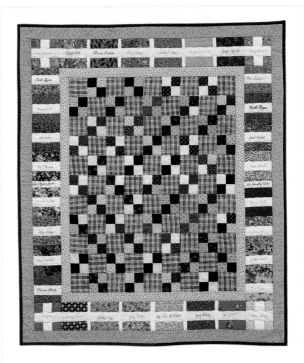

Friendship Quilt *by Dori Hawks, 1999, Salem, South Carolina, 42¾" x 49". Dori put some leftover four patches to use, creating a gentle beige palette and a homespun look. Rail Fence and Nine Patch Variation blocks form the border.*

Snowball Blocks

Method One

Use this method to make blocks from yardage. It yields 8 blocks, each finishing 4½" square (5" unfinished).

1. From muslin or other light signature fabric, cut 1 strip, 5" x 42". Crosscut into 8 squares, each 5" x 5".

2. From print fabric, cut 2 strips, 2" x 42". Print strips may be cut from the same fabric or from 2 different prints. Crosscut into 32 squares, each 2" x 2".

3. Use a mechanical pencil to draw a light diagonal line from corner to corner on the wrong side of each 2" print square. With right sides together, place a marked print square on each corner of a 5" signature square, and sew directly on the diagonal line as shown. Trim the corners, leaving a ¼"-wide seam allowance. Gently press the corners toward the print triangles. Make 8 blocks.

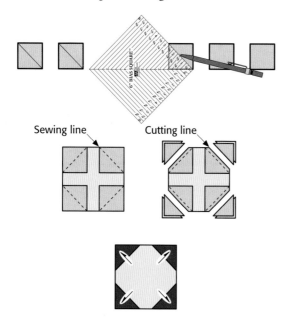

Sewing line · Cutting line

Method Two

Use this method to make blocks from scraps. It yields 1 block, finishing 4½" square (5" unfinished).

1. From muslin or other light signature fabric, cut 1 square, 5" x 5". From print scraps, cut 4 squares, each 2" x 2".

2. Complete the block as directed in "Method One," step 3, above.

Diagonal Strip Blocks

Instructions for the projects in this book use Method Two for constructing the Diagonal Strip blocks. This method involves cutting the strips on the straight of grain, which makes more economical use of the fabric. Note, however, that this method results in blocks whose outside edges finish on the bias, so handle the completed blocks carefully!

Method One

Use this method to make blocks from yardage and when you prefer to work with strips cut on the bias. It yields 10 blocks, each finishing 4½" square (5" unfinished).

> *Method One involves cutting the strips on the bias and is offered as an option for those who prefer the outside edges of each block to finish on the straight of grain. If you choose this method, you will need to adjust the amounts of fabric given in the materials list to accommodate the bias strips.*

1. Fold and crease a fat quarter of signature fabric on the diagonal as shown, and cut on that diagonal line. Remove the selvage, and sew the 2 sections together on the selvage ends as shown.

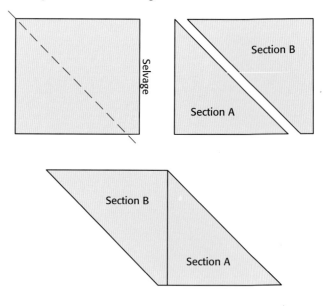

2. Rotate the fabric so that the diagonal cut line is parallel with the vertical lines on your cutting mat. Fold the top triangle point down, keeping the left edges aligned. Fold the bottom triangle point up, keeping the right edges aligned. It doesn't matter how far you fold the points, but both new folds should be parallel with the horizontal lines on your cutting mat.

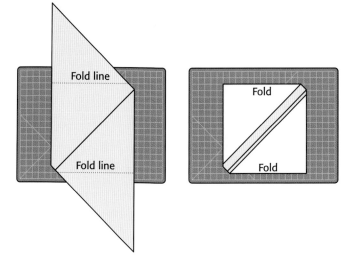

3. Repeat steps 1 and 2 to cut, piece, and fold similar units from 2 or 4 different print fabrics, depending on how scrappy you'd like the block to be.

4. Cut 4 strips, each 1⅟₁₆"-wide, from the folded signature fabric; piece them in pairs to make a total of 2 strips, each 1⅟₁₆" x 50" (approximate). Cut a total of 8 strips, each 1⅟₁₆" wide, from the folded print fabrics; piece them in pairs to make a total of 4 strips, each one 1⅟₁₆" x 50" (approximate). Trim the pointed ends of each pieced strip as shown.

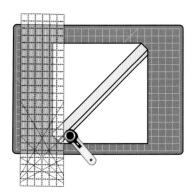

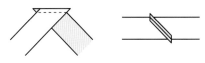

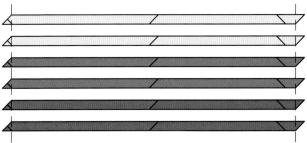

Joining bias strips

5. Sew one 1⅟₁₆"-wide signature strip between two 1⅟₁₆"-wide print strips to make a strip set that measures 3⅟₁₆" x 42". Press seams toward the print strips. Make 2 strip sets.

Make 2.

6. With right sides together, stitch the 2 strip sets from step 5 together along both long, raw edges to make a tube.

7. Place the tube on your cutting mat, aligning the raw edges of a seam sewn in step 6 with a horizontal line on the mat. Trim one end of the tube at a 45° angle, using your quilter's ruler and the 45° diagonal line on your mat as a guide.

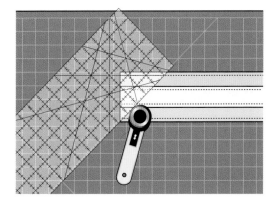

8. Place your Bias Square ruler on the tube so that the 5" line is directly on top of the 45° cut you made in step 7, and the diagonal line on the ruler is aligned with the tube's bottom seam line. Complete the triangle by cutting along the edge of the Bias Square as shown.

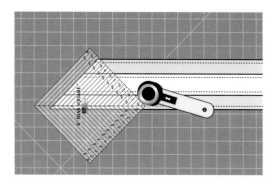

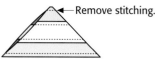

9. Use a seam ripper to remove the bit of machine stitching on the point of the double-thickness triangle, and open it out into a 5" square. Press the center seam open.

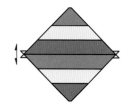

You'll notice that 2 corners of the square are "nipped off," but this blunt edge will be sewn into the seam allowance when the block is joined to other blocks in your quilt.

10. Without changing the orientation of the Bias Square ruler, slide it so the 5" line on the bottom half of the square is directly on top of the cut you made in step 8, and the ruler's diagonal line is aligned with the top seam line on the tube. Complete another triangle by cutting along the edge of the Bias Square. Remove the bit of

machine stitching, open the square, and press as described in step 9.

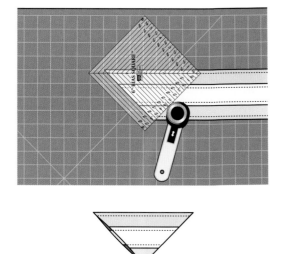

11. Repeat steps 7–10 to make a total of 10 blocks.

Method Two

Use this method to make blocks from yardage and when you prefer to work with strips cut on the straight of grain (see "Rotary Cutting," steps 1–3, on page 8). It yields 10 blocks, each finishing 4½" square (5" unfinished).

1. Cut 2 strips, each 1⁹⁄₁₆" x 42", from the signature fabric; cut a total of 4 strips, each 1⁹⁄₁₆" x 42", from 2 or 4 different print fabrics, depending on how scrappy you'd like the block to be.

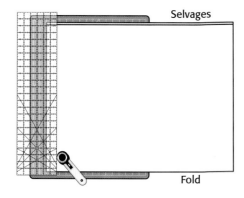

2. Continue as directed in "Diagonal Strip Blocks," steps 5–11, Method One to create strip sets and tubes that are on the straight of grain rather than the bias. Make 10 blocks.

Method Three

Use this method to make blocks from scraps. It yields 1 block, finishing 4½" square (5" unfinished).

1. You may wish to cut all strips on the straight of grain or all of them on the bias, but you should be consistent. Cut 2 strips, each 1⁹⁄₁₆" x 8", from the signature fabric; cut a total of 4 strips, each 1⁹⁄₁₆" x 8", from print scraps.

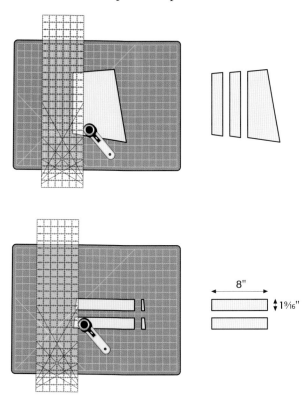

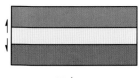

2. Sew one 1⁹⁄₁₆" x 8" signature strip between two 1⁹⁄₁₆" x 8" print strips to make a strip set that measures 3¹¹⁄₁₆" x 8". Press seams toward the print strips. Make 2 strip sets.

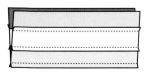

Make 2.

3. With right sides together, stitch the 2 strip sets from step 2 together along one long, raw edge. Do not unfold the strip sets.

4. Place the stitched unit from step 3 on your cutting mat, aligning the raw edge of the seam sewn in step 3 with a horizontal line on the mat as shown. Trim one end of the strip set at a 45° angle, using your quilter's ruler and the 45° diagonal line on your mat as a guide.

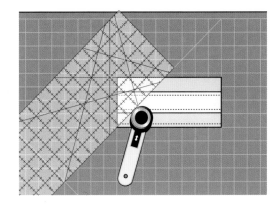

5. Place your Bias Square ruler on the strip set so that the 5" line is directly on top of the 45° cut you made in step 4, and the diagonal line on the ruler is aligned with the seam line sewn in step 3. Complete the triangle by cutting along the edge of the Bias Square as shown. Open the triangle out into a 5" square, and press the center seam open.

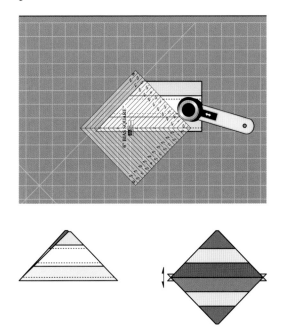

Writing on the Blocks

Preparing the Blocks

Prepare the blocks for signatures or other lettering by stabilizing the signature fabric with freezer paper. Cut the freezer paper slightly smaller than the signature surface; this will encourage signers to stay comfortably within the confines of the signature fabric and enable you to sew the blocks together with no difficulty. For each Rail Fence and Nine Patch Variation block, cut a 1¼" x 4" strip of freezer paper. For each Snowball block, cut a 4" x 4" square of freezer paper. For each Diagonal Strip block, cut two 1" x 3½" strips of freezer paper.

Press the appropriate size and shape of freezer paper, shiny side down, to the wrong side of the signature fabric in each block.

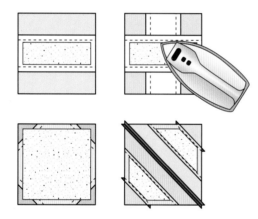

If you wish, cut trapezoid-shaped strips of freezer paper for Diagonal Strip blocks. Use your rotary cutter, quilter's ruler, and the 45° line on your cutting mat to trim the corners of each 1" x 3½" freezer-paper strip.

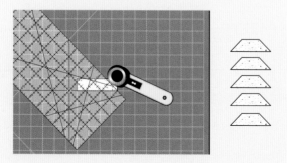

Gathering Signatures

When you distribute your blocks for signing, allow each signer to practice first on a fabric sample that you have stabilized with freezer paper. This will give the signer a feel for the process, minimizing errors and the resulting wasted blocks. If, after you have collected the signed blocks, you are concerned that the signatures will not show up clearly on your quilt, you may want to darken them. While doing so, you may decide to straighten some of the loops and lines for more conformity. I took this liberty with the signatures of my guild friends so that the signatures were more visible from a distance and played a more important role in the quilt design. Pale signatures do not stand up well on a vibrant background of pretty fabrics.

Sally Collins

Sally Collins

Sally Collins

Artistic Lettering

I think of calligraphy as stylish penmanship, while lettering entails drawing individual pictures of the alphabetic characters. Consider each individual letter or number as an item to sketch, rather than viewing the entire grouping as a word to write.

An entire set of alphabetic and numeric characters in a particular style is called a *font*. Each font has its own defining elements. Certain fonts have little strokes, called *serifs*, at the end of vertical or diagonal lines in each letter. Some lettering, called *italic*, features a uniform slant; another has bold or thick lines, and so on. I've included a variety of fonts in this book to give you some suggestions (see page 18). Examine these, the fonts available on your computer, or those appearing in various publications to understand the elements of lettering styles.

Sometimes you are the one to do the lettering on your quilt, or you may be called upon to sign a block for someone else. First, you'll need to select a font. Review the various alphabets I've included on page 18, or print out some words using the various fonts on your computer to see which ones best suit your style or your quilt plan. Look at the name Old King Cole on "Mother Goose and Friends" on page 41. I printed it out from my word processor using a Gothic-style font, which seemed appropriate for the style and theme of the quilt. With the printout as a guide, I copied the wording onto the signature fabric one letter at a time.

Computer-generated lettering

Once you've settled on a font, practice writing your name—or the desired words and/or phrases—in that font on an appropriately sized piece of plain paper. This allows you to experiment a bit and to see how the lettering fills the available area most evenly. Keep in mind that all the letters do not take up the same physical space. For example, an *i* is considerably narrower than an *m*.

Some alphabetic characters fit closely enough together that there is very little "white space" between the letters of a word. Note the differences in white spaces among the various letters below as they are produced by typing on my computer.

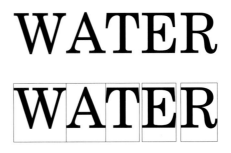

On the other hand, when I'm lettering by hand, the *W*, *A*, and *T* can be "squeezed together" to eliminate excess white space in the word. These letters may actually overlap each other's space a bit. Now the letters appear more evenly spaced, although we can see that, in reality, they are not.

As you practice your lettering, notice the strokes or forms common to the font you have chosen. These elements will be repeated in many of the alphanumeric characters you have chosen to write in that style.

A B D F H I J K L P Q R T Y Z

B T

ABCDEFGHIJKLMNOPQRS
TUVWXYZabcdefghijklmnop
qrstuvwxyz1234567890

ABCDEFGHIJKLMNOP2RST
UVWXYZabcdefghijklmnopqrstuv
wxyz1234567890

ABCDEFGHIJKLMNOPQRST
UVWXYZabcdefghijklmno
pqrstuvwxyz1234567890

**ABCDEFGHIJKLMNOPQR
STUVWXYZabcdefghijkl
mnopqrstuvwxyz1234567
890**

ABCDEFGHIJKLMNOPQRSTUVWXYZ123
4567890

ABCDEFGHIJKLMNOPQR
STUVWXYZabcdefghijklmnop
qrstuvwxyz1234567890

Once you feel comfortable with the font and the spacing, you are ready to write on the signature fabric. Using a mechanical pencil, lightly sketch the letters and words within the stabilized signature area. Then use permanent pens to "create" each individual letter (see "Pens" on page 6).

As you proceed, start making artistic decisions. For example, consider using one color (black) at the top of the letters, and another (red) at the bottom.

two-toned lettering

Or, you may wish to vary the thickness of the lines within the letters. It is most common to use finer lines on the diagonal strokes and upstrokes, and heavier lines on the downstrokes. This "rule of thumb" dates back to the era of the quill pen, which automatically created this effect. For additional guidance, examine similar fonts in books and newspapers, or on your computer to see which lines of a particular letter would be heavy and which lines would be fine. Then carefully go over the heavier lines in your lettering with additional pen strokes until you achieve the desired thickness.

If your lettering becomes too heavy, you may need to retrace the lightest letters until they are all of a consistent density. This process is also handy for disguising minor imperfections in your original lettering.

Thick and Thin
Thick and Thin

If you complete a word and are not satisfied with the workmanship, keep going! You can add an uneven underline, place balloons or flowers in the background for balance, purposely change the thickness of letters from left to right, or shadow entire words. Allow yourself to have a loose drawing experience, and you may be more pleased with the result than if you were to be mechanically and technically perfect from start to finish.

Example of a poorly centered, careless signature

Artwork added to disguise the
poor balance and uneven style

Heat-Setting the Ink

Before continuing with the construction of the quilt, follow the instructions provided by the pen manufacturer to heat-set the writing on each block. Heat-setting usually entails thoroughly pressing the lettering with a hot iron to ensure that the ink doesn't fade or bleed.

Putting It Together

Arranging Your Blocks

If your blocks are the result of an exchange, you will probably have an interesting collection of colors and fabrics that, at first glance, don't seem to relate to each other. One block may be royal blue, another pale turquoise, and yet another a brown-and-black floral. A good trick for creating balance in your quilt top is to scatter the strongest colors. Place brights, such as red or aqua, throughout the set, rather than concentrating them in just one area, so they do not dominate the other, less flashy colors.

At the same time, if you have blocks in an assortment of patterns, try them in a variety of arrangements until you find one that creates a pleasing visual balance and possibly an interesting secondary design. Refer to the various examples in this book for inspiration. Some of the photos show quilts made with only one or two block types, some with three of the choices, and others with all four block designs.

Choosing the Sashing

Many setting possibilities for your friendship blocks will involve the use of sashing and borders, so the next challenge is to select sashing or border fabrics that tie in and complement the exchange blocks. As you study the various examples in this book, you will realize that there are many options. By their very nature, most friendship quilts are scrappy to some extent, and it's hard to make a mistake with scrap quilts if you spend a few moments with your blocks and fabric stash. Refer to *Scrap Frenzy* by Sally Schneider (Martingale & Company, 2001) as an excellent reference on this subject.

If the fabrics in your signature blocks are of mostly medium values, you may elect to create sashing that is darker to show off the geometry of the blocks and setting. In other instances, a more subtle contrast may suit you.

Almost every project in this book can be made with any combination of the four block types. The sashing choice is what makes each quilt unique.

Geometric elements common to several of the sashing suggestions in this book are the half-square-triangle, the quarter-square-triangle, and the 60°-triangle blocks. These units can be combined with other compatibly sized squares, strips, and rectangles for dramatic and pleasing effects.

Half-Square-Triangle Blocks

Half-square-triangle blocks are constructed from fabric squares cut 7/8" larger than the desired finished blocks. For the various projects in this book, the finished half-square-triangle block will measure 1½" x 1½", so the fabric squares are cut 2⅜" x 2⅜". If you wish to alter the size of the half-square-triangle blocks, just add 7/8" to the desired finished size of the block to determine the cut dimensions of the fabric squares.

1. Cut 1 square, 2⅜" x 2⅜", from 2 contrasting (e.g., light and dark) fabrics. Use a mechanical pencil to draw a diagonal line from corner to corner on the wrong side of the lighter square.

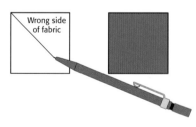

Wrong side of fabric

2. Place the squares right sides together with the lighter, marked square on top. Stitch a scant ¼" from each side of the pencil line, then cut directly on the pencil line. Unfold the pieced units and press seams toward the darker triangles. If necessary, trim the completed half-square-triangle

blocks to 2" x 2". You will have 2 half-square-triangle blocks.

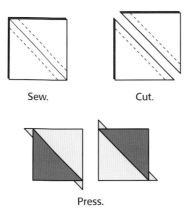

Sew.   Cut.

Press.

Quarter-Square-Triangle Blocks

Quarter-square-triangle blocks are constructed from fabric squares cut 1¼" larger than the desired finished block. For the various projects in this book, the finished quarter-square-triangle block will measure 1½" x 1½", so the fabric squares are cut 2¾" x 2¾". If you wish to alter the size of the quarter-square-triangle blocks, just add 1¼" to the desired finished size of the block to determine the cut dimensions of the fabric squares.

1. Cut 1 square, 2¾" x 2¾", from 2 contrasting (e.g., light and dark) fabrics. Use these squares to construct a pair of large half-square-triangle units as described in "Half-Square-Triangle Blocks" on page 20 and above. *Do not* trim the units at this point.

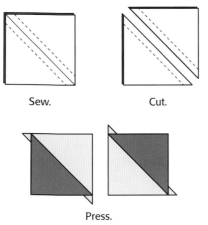

Sew.   Cut.

Press.

2. Use a mechanical pencil to draw a diagonal line from corner to corner on the wrong side of one half-square-triangle unit. Place the squares right sides together, with opposite colors touching and with the marked square on top. Stitch a scant ¼" from each side of the new pencil line.

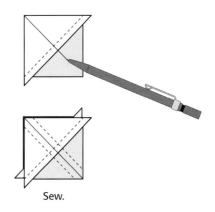

Sew.

3. Cut directly on the pencil line. Unfold the pieced units and press the seams open. If necessary, trim the completed quarter-square-triangle blocks to 2" x 2". You will have 2 quarter-square-triangle blocks.

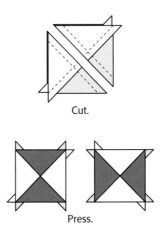

Cut.

Press.

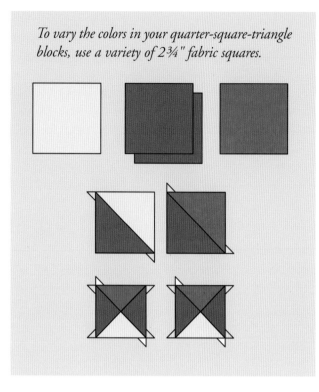

To vary the colors in your quarter-square-triangle blocks, use a variety of 2¾" fabric squares.

Combination-Square-Triangle Blocks

Combination-square-triangle blocks combine the look and construction techniques of the half- and quarter-square-triangle blocks.

1. Cut 1 square, 2¾" x 2¾", from 2 contrasting (e.g., light and dark) fabrics. Use these squares to construct a pair of large half-square-triangle units as described in "Half-Square-Triangle Blocks" on pages 20–21. *Do not* trim the units at this point.

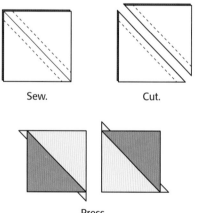

Sew. Cut.

Press.

2. Cut 2 squares, each 2⅜" x 2⅜", from the darker fabric. Use a mechanical pencil to draw a line from corner to corner on the wrong side of each square.

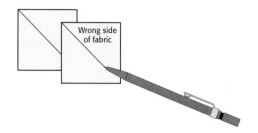

3. Place each 2⅜" dark fabric square and a half-square-triangle unit from step 1 right sides together. Be sure the dark, marked square is on top, with the diagonal pencil line positioned in the opposite direction from the diagonal seam in the pieced unit beneath it. Stitch a scant ¼" from each side of the pencil line.

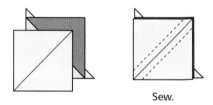

Sew.

4. Cut directly on the pencil line. Unfold the units and press seams to one side. If necessary, trim the completed blocks to 2" x 2". You will have 4 combination-square-triangle blocks.

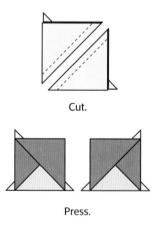

Cut.

Press.

– 22 –

60°-Triangle Blocks

With 60°-triangle blocks, you can create lovely star effects in your sashing. To emphasize this effect and for a crisp, clean secondary pattern, use the same fabric you plan to use for cornerstones for the single, wide triangle; use sashing fabric for the two long, skinny triangles. For an exciting alternative, select a random variety of fabrics.

There are various tools on the market that can ease the cutting and construction of these blocks. However, for our purposes, it is just as convenient to create them using paper-piecing techniques.

1. Trace the block below onto paper to use as the foundation. Cut out the traced block, leaving a little extra margin of paper around the outside edges.

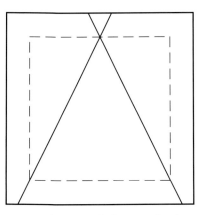

Pattern for paper piecing 60° triangles

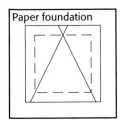

2. Place a scrap of your "wide triangle" fabric under the foundation, wrong side toward the paper. Make sure that the scrap is large enough to cover the triangle shape, plus the approximately ¼"-wide seam allowance around it. Secure the scrap to the foundation with 1 or 2 pins.

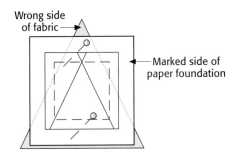

3. Position and pin an oversized scrap of "skinny triangle" fabric right side up under the foundation as shown. Be sure that the scrap is large enough so that when the seam is completed, the fabric can be folded back to cover the corner of the block, plus the outer seam allowance.

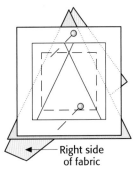

4. Set your sewing machine to sew a small stitch (e.g., 12 to 14 stitches per inch), and sew directly on the sewing line you've marked on the paper foundation. Fold the paper pattern back along the sewn seam line, exposing the excess fabric beneath. Trim the fabric, leaving a ¼"-wide seam allowance as shown.

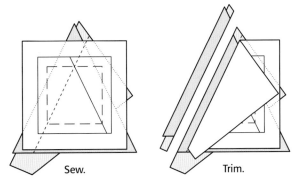

5. Turn the piece over and unfold the newly sewn skinny triangle piece toward the corner of the block. Finger-press it in place, making sure that it covers the whole corner of the paper foundation.

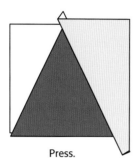

Press.

6. Repeat steps 3–5 to cover the opposite corner of the paper foundation.

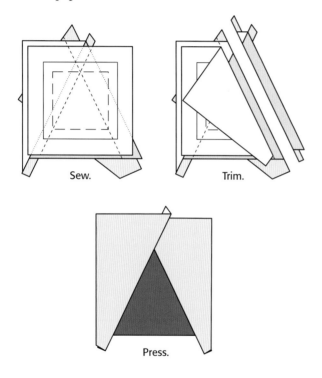

Sew.

Trim.

Press.

7. With the paper side up, trim away the excess fabric and foundation, leaving a 2" square.

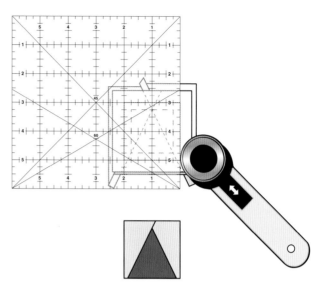

8. Remove the paper carefully by tearing it gently along the seam lines.

Variety Sashing

The various triangle-based blocks described on pages 20–24 may be combined with simple 2" squares to create a wide variety of exciting and original sashing options. All of these elements finish to 1½" square, so three of them can be sewn together to create 4½"-long finished sashing strips, perfectly matching the finished dimensions of the various signature blocks.

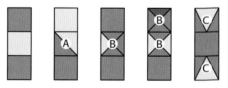

A = half-square-triangle block
B = quarter-square-triangle block
or combination-square-triangle block
C = 60°-triangle block

Many of the quilts pictured in this book have very formal, balanced sashing designs.

Sometimes, however, to complement a random, scrappy quilt top, it is nice to create sashing with a correspondingly free-spirited style. In this case, consider introducing asymmetrical elements into your sashing, arranging them to balance the block layout in your set, as shown in the illustration below and in the quilt "Wordsmiths" on page 59.

Balanced sashing

Sashing with asymmetrical elements

Lake and Mountain Friends by Bonnie B. Ouellette, 2000, Seneca, South Carolina, 79" x 79". Rather than set her blocks with sashing, Bonnie surrounded a central block with a dynamic series of borders. All the border choices work perfectly, adding sparkle and unifying the different elements in this quilted treasure.

Finishing Your Project

Choosing a Quilting Design

Before you sandwich and baste the layers (quilt top, batting, and backing) of your quilt, select quilting designs that are compatible with the geometric features of your quilt top. One option is for the quilting lines to follow and echo the seams in your piece. You might outline quilt by stitching ¼" from the seam lines of the various shapes, or quilt in the ditch by stitching right alongside the seam lines.

You can also add excitement to your piece by introducing quilting lines that carry the eye in new directions. Stippling or quilting between the design elements adds interest, while also helping to fill in empty space.

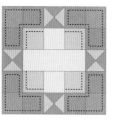
Outline quilting

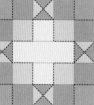
Quilting in the ditch

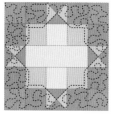
Stippling

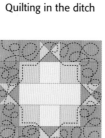
Meandering

The most interesting quilts combine a variety of quilting approaches. In addition to trying outline and in-the-ditch stitching, loops, and stippling, you may want to select stencils of suitable size and design to introduce curved lines to your otherwise straight-line quilt top (see "Nauti-Thoughts" on page 64). Precut stencils are found in fabric stores, by mail order, and at vendors' booths at quilt expositions. You can also cut your own stencils with a sheet of plastic template material and a utility knife.

If you are planning to outline your quilt elements with parallel or in-the-ditch stitching, you won't need to mark these quilting designs. You may also feel confident enough to free-motion quilt stippling and loops without the aid of marked guidelines. However, other quilting motifs will need to be marked on the quilt top.

Whether you plan to quilt by hand or by machine, mark your quilt top before you put the layers together. There are many marking tools available: a regular No. 2 or No. 3 pencil, a fine-lead mechanical pencil, or any of a variety of chalk markers are all suitable options. Whichever marking method you choose, test it first on scraps of the fabric you've used in your quilt. Check for three factors: you'll want the marks to be visible, they should remain visible throughout the quilting process, and they should be easy to remove.

A light box is handy for tracing quilt designs onto fabric. If you don't have a light box, you can tape the design onto a window, tape the fabric over the design, and trace the motifs onto the fabric.

Sandwiching the Layers

1. Press the quilt backing fabric. It should be approximately 2" larger than the constructed quilt top on each side.
2. Use masking tape to secure the backing fabric, wrong side up, on a smooth, clean surface.
3. Center the batting over the backing and smooth it in place, making sure not to stretch the batting.
4. Carefully center the quilt top, right side up, over the batting and smooth out any unevenness.

If you plan to machine quilt the project, use rust-proof safety pins to secure the layers together, placing pins approximately 6" apart.

If you are planning to hand quilt, thread-baste the layers together. Pin the layers first with long quilter's pins; then use a long needle and sturdy thread to make long running stitches. A contrasting-color thread makes the stitches easy to see; however, avoid very dark thread on light fabrics. The thread might leave dots of dye residue when the stitches are removed.

Start in the center of the secured layers, stitching parallel to the sides of the quilt to form a grid of lines about 4" to 5" apart. Finish by basting around the quilt top's outer edges.

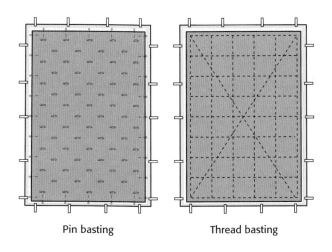

Pin basting   Thread basting

Quilting Your Project

Hand Quilting

You will need short, sturdy needles called Betweens, quilting thread, and a thimble for the middle finger of your sewing hand. For the smallest stitches, use the smallest needle you can comfortably handle. An excellent resource on hand quilting is *Loving Stitches: A Guide to Fine Hand Quilting* by Jeana Kimball (That Patchwork Place, 1992).

Machine Quilting

For straight-line quilting, it is very important that the layers of your quilt feed through the machine without any puckering or shifting. If your machine does not feature an even-feed mechanism, a walking-foot attachment will alleviate that potential problem. Easing the downward tension of your presser foot is also an option on some older machine models.

Walking foot

For free-motion quilting, you must drop or cover the feed dogs on your machine and attach a darning foot or similar attachment. This enables you to guide the quilt freely and to follow the direction of the quilting design, instead of turning the fabric under the needle. Use this method to outline motifs in the fabric, to add stippling or loops, and to follow the lines of other curved designs.

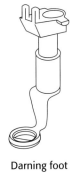

Darning foot

Binding and Labeling

Prepare your quilt for binding by trimming away most of the excess batting and backing. Unless otherwise directed, leave a margin of batting and backing equal to the desired width of the binding minus ¼". For instance, if you want binding that measures ¾" wide, trim the batting and backing so that ½" remains past the edge of your pieced top.

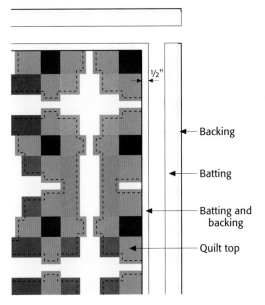

Trim batting and backing
½" from edge of quilt top.

Follow these directions for double-fold bias binding.

1. Fold the binding fabric as shown, paying careful attention to the location of the lettered corners.

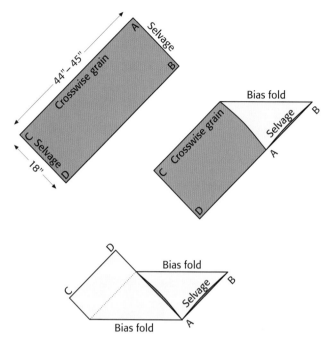

2. Cut strips perpendicular to the folds as shown and according to the chart below.

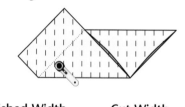

Finished Width of Binding	Cut Width of Bias Strips
¼"	1¾"
⅜"	2¼"
½"	2¾"
¾"	3¾"
1"	4¾"

3. With right sides together, join strip segments at right angles and stitch across the corner as shown. Trim any excess seam allowance to ¼" and press seams open to make one long piece of binding.

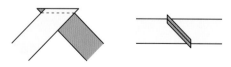

4. Turn under ¼" at the beginning of the binding strip and press. Fold the binding in half lengthwise, wrong sides together; press. Trim the "dog ears" from the seams as shown.

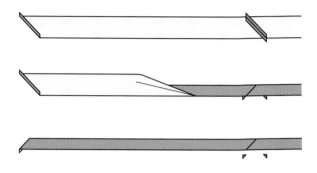

5. Starting on one side of the quilt (not a corner), and leaving the first 5" unsewn, stitch the binding to the quilt with a ¼"-wide seam. Keep the raw edges of the binding even with the raw edges of the quilt top. End the stitching the same distance from the first corner as the width of your finished binding. For example, if your finished binding will be ¾" wide, stop sewing ¾" from the corner. Backstitch and clip the thread.

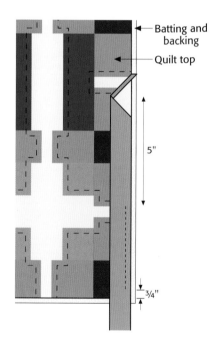

6. Turn the quilt so you will be stitching down the next edge. Fold the binding up, away from the quilt, aligning raw edges with the quilt top. Then fold the binding back down onto itself, creating a fold parallel to the quilt top and even with the edges of the batting and backing.

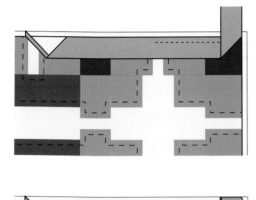

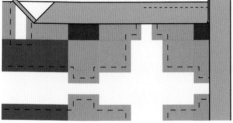

7. Begin sewing at the edge of the binding, back-stitching to secure and taking a ¼"-wide seam. Your new line of stitching should touch the end of the previous stitching on the back of the quilt.

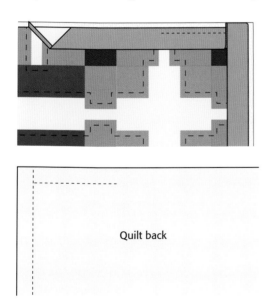

Quilt back

8. Repeat the process on the remaining edges and corners of the quilt. As you approach the starting point of the binding, stop stitching. Overlap the starting edge by about 1", and trim the excess binding at a 45° angle. Tuck the end of the binding into the fold and finish the seam.

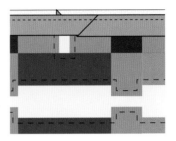

9. Fold the binding over the raw edges to the back of the quilt, covering the line of machine stitching, and pin in place. Use matching-color thread to blindstitch the binding to the back of the quilt. A miter will form at each corner. Blindstitch the mitered corners in place by hand stitching the diagonal fold.

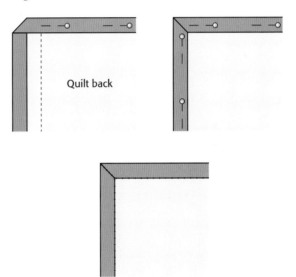

Quilt back

10. Make a label for the quilt. Include such information as your name, address, and date. Include any story connected with the making of the quilt, such as the recipient, a related special occasion, or recognition of anyone who helped with the creation. Use permanent pen or machine embroidery on muslin or other almost-solid fabric. Sew the label to the back of the finished quilt.

Track and Trail

By Marge Edie, 2001, Clemson, South Carolina, 32½" x 46½".

As I designed this quilt on the computer, I could see paths taking shape across the quilt, so I constructed the squares out of earth-colored prints and invited our local running club to sign them. The areas of unsigned squares are free-motion quilted in forest-floor leaves.

Featuring the Rail Fence, Nine Patch Variation, and Diagonal Strip blocks, this quilt is a wonderful vehicle for a block exchange. There is an endless variety of settings possible for these blocks, and all create interesting pathways to follow.

My decision here was to checkerboard the Diagonal Strip blocks, pointing them in random directions, and fill in with the Rail Fence and Nine Patch Variation blocks, but this is not required. Try various arrangements with your blocks until you get the look you want.

Materials

Yardage based on 42"-wide fabric unless otherwise stated.
1 yd. muslin or other light fabric for signature strips
1⅜ yds. *total* of assorted medium green, brown, and gold prints for blocks
⅛ yd. brown print for border
½ yd. earth-colored print for binding
1½ yds. fabric for backing
37" x 51" piece of batting

Cutting

All measurements include ¼"-wide seam allowances.
From the muslin or other light (signature) fabric, cut:
- 9 strips, each 2" x 20", for Rail Fence and Nine Patch Variation blocks

- 18 rectangles, each 2" x 5", for Nine Patch Variation blocks

- 1 square, 5" x 5", for Snowball block

From the assorted medium green, brown, and gold prints, cut a *total* of:
- 18 strips, each 2" x 20", for Rail Fence and Nine Patch Variation blocks

- 4 squares, each 2" x 2", for Snowball block

From the brown print, cut:
- 4 strips, each ¾" x 42", for border

Cutting for the Diagonal Strip Blocks

In addition to cutting the strips indicated in the cutting instructions at left, you'll need to cut the following strips for the Diagonal Strip blocks. To make the most economical use of fabric, cut the strips on the straight grain of the fabric, referring to Method Two for "Diagonal Strip Blocks" on page 14.

Fabric	Total No. of Strips	Strip Width	Strip Length
Muslin or other light (signature) fabric	8	1⁹⁄₁₆"	42"
Assorted medium green, brown, and gold prints	16	1⁹⁄₁₆"	42"

Making the Blocks

1. Refer to step 2 of Method One for "Rail Fence Blocks" on page 10. Use the 9 muslin or other light 2" x 20" strips and the 18 assorted medium green, brown, and gold 2" x 20" strips to make a total of 9 Rail Fence strip sets, each measuring 5" x 20".

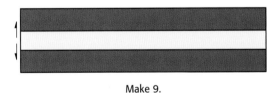

Make 9.

2. From each of the 9 strip sets, crosscut two 5" segments to use as Rail Fence blocks and four 2" segments to use in the construction of the Nine Patch Variation blocks. You'll have a total of 18 Rail Fence blocks and 36 Nine Patch segments. Set 1 Rail Fence block aside for another project.

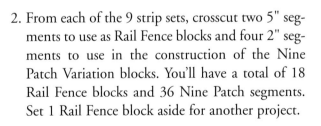

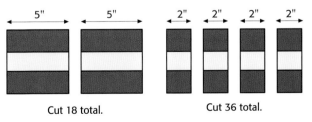

Cut 18 total.   Cut 36 total.

3. Refer to step 2 of Method One for "Nine Patch Variation Blocks" on page 11. Use the 18 muslin or other light 2" x 5" rectangles and the 36 Nine Patch 2"-wide segments from step 2 to make a total of 18 Nine Patch Variation blocks. Set 1 block aside for another project.

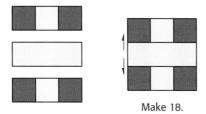

Make 18.

4. Refer to Method Two for "Diagonal Strip Blocks" on page 14. Use the 8 muslin or other light 1⅛6" x 42" strips and the 16 assorted medium green, brown, and gold 1⅛6" x 42" strips to make a total of 8 strip sets.

Make 8.

5. Sew the strip sets from step 4 in pairs to make 4 strip-set tubes. Use the tubes to make a total of 35 Diagonal Strip blocks.

Make 4.

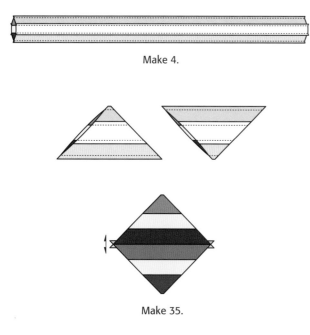

Make 35.

6. Refer to Method Two for "Snowball Blocks" on page 12. Use the 5" muslin or other light square and the 4 assorted medium green, brown, and gold 2" squares to make 1 Snowball block.

Make 1.

Adding the Lettering

1. Refer to "Writing on the Blocks" on page 16. Prepare each block for signature by pressing an appropriately sized strip of freezer paper to the reverse side of the signature area.
2. Distribute the Rail Fence, Nine Patch Variation, and Diagonal Strip blocks for signatures. When the blocks are returned to you, refer to "Artistic Lettering" on page 16 and augment the signatures as desired. Heat-set the ink as described on page 19.
3. Letter the name of the group or any other special information onto the Snowball block.

Assembling the Quilt Top

1. Refer to "Arranging Your Blocks" on page 20. Lay out the blocks in 10 horizontal rows of 7 blocks each as shown in the assembly diagram below. Refer to the quilt photo on page 30 for additional guidance.

2. Sew the blocks together into horizontal rows. Press seams in opposite directions from row to row.

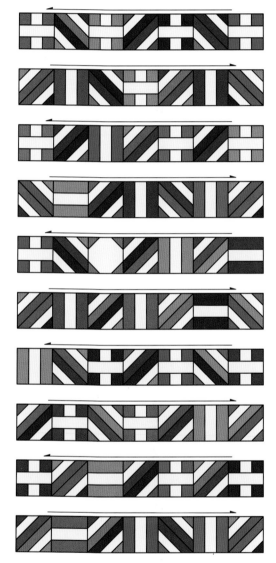

Assembly Diagram

3. With right sides together and long, raw edges aligned, pin the rows together carefully, matching the seams; stitch. Press as desired.

4. Join the ¾" x 42" brown print border strips end to end to make a continuous ¾"-wide strip. Measure the quilt through its horizontal center, and cut 2 border strips to this measurement from the ¾"-wide strip. Mark the center of the quilt edges and the border strips. With right sides together and long, raw edges aligned, pin the trimmed borders to the top and bottom of the quilt top, matching the center marks and ends and easing as necessary. Press seams toward the borders.

5. Measure the quilt through its vertical center, including the borders you've just added. Cut 2 border strips to this measurement from the remaining ¾"-wide strip, and follow the procedure described in step 4 to add these border strips to the sides of the quilt; press.

Finishing

Refer to "Finishing Your Project" on pages 26–29 for guidance as needed.

1. Select a quilting design and mark the quilt top as necessary.

2. Center the quilt top and batting over the backing; pin or thread-baste.

3. Hand or machine quilt as desired.

4. Trim the batting and backing as instructed in "Binding and Labeling" on page 27. Use the ½ yard of earth-colored print to cut a total of 180" of 2¾"-wide bias binding strips. Use the strips to construct a double-fold bias binding (to finish ½" wide). Sew the binding to the quilt.

5. Make a label and attach it to your quilt.

Blue Suede

By Marge Edie, 2000, Clemson, South Carolina, 32½" x 32½".

These soft tones appeared very leathery, so I used the large copper star sequins to further the feeling of unusual materials for a quilt. As you can see, these geometries, while perfect for signature quilts, can be just as attractive for other projects.

"Blue Suede" features the Rail Fence and Nine Patch Variation blocks, but you may decide to include any of the four block types that appeal to your creative instincts. Notice, for example, that in a similar quilt, "Plenty" (below), I used three of the four block types: the two included here and Snowball.

Varying the block arrangement and sashing design adds to the creative possibilities. In "Plenty," a narrower sashing results in a tighter-looking grid.

Plenty *by Marge Edie, 2000, Clemson, South Carolina, 20¾" x 31".*

Materials

Yardage based on 42"-wide fabric unless otherwise stated.

½ yd. muslin or other light fabric for signature strips and sashing

⅜ yd. *total* of assorted medium blue print scraps for blocks

½ yd. gold print for sashing

¼ yd. red print for cornerstones

1⅛ yds. fabric for backing

⅜ yd. blue print for binding

37" x 37" square of batting

Cutting

All measurements include ¼"-wide seam allowances.

From the muslin or other light (signature) fabric, cut:

- 25 rectangles, each 2" x 5", for Rail Fence and Nine Patch Variation blocks

- 13 rectangles, each 2" x 4", for Nine Patch Variation blocks

- 3 strips, each 1" x 42", for sashing

From the assorted medium blue print scraps, cut a *total* of:

- 24 rectangles, each 2" x 5", for Rail Fence blocks

- 26 rectangles, each 2" x 4", for Nine Patch Variation blocks

From the gold print, cut:

- 6 strips, each 2½" x 42", for sashing

From the red print, cut:

- 36 squares, each 2" x 2", for cornerstones

Making the Blocks

1. Refer to Method Two for "Rail Fence Blocks" on page 10. Use 12 muslin or other light 2" x 5" rectangles and the 24 medium blue 2" x 5" rectangles to make a total of 12 Rail Fence blocks.

Make 12.

2. Refer to Method Two for "Nine Patch Variation Blocks" on page 11. Use the remaining 13 muslin or other light 2" x 5" rectangles, the 13 muslin or other light 2" x 4" rectangles, and the 26 assorted medium blue 2" x 4" rectangles to make a total of 13 Nine Patch Variation blocks.

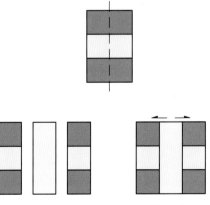

Make 13.

Adding the Lettering

1. Refer to "Writing on the Blocks" on page 16. Prepare each block for signature by pressing an appropriately sized strip of freezer paper to the reverse side of the signature area.

2. Distribute the blocks for signatures. When the blocks are returned to you, refer to "Artistic Lettering" on page 16 and augment the signatures as desired. Heat-set the ink as described on page 19.

Assembling the Quilt Top

1. Sew a 1" x 42" muslin strip between two 2½" x 42" gold print strips to make a strip set measuring 5" x 42". Press seams toward the gold print strips. Make 3 strip sets.

2. Crosscut the strip sets into a total of 60 segments, each 2" wide, for sashing units.

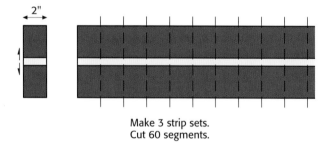

Make 3 strip sets.
Cut 60 segments.

3. Refer to "Arranging Your Blocks" on page 20. Lay out the blocks and sashing units in 5 horizontal rows, alternating 6 sashing units and 5 blocks in each row. Refer to the assembly diagram at right and the quilt photo on page 34 for guidance as necessary.

4. Sew the blocks and sashing units together into horizontal rows. Press seams toward the sashing units.

5. Arrange and sew 6 red print 2" cornerstones and 5 sashing units in a horizontal row as shown. Press seams toward the sashing units. Make 6 rows.

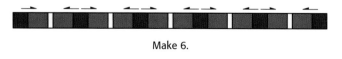

Make 6.

6. Lay out the rows, alternating them as shown in the assembly diagram. With right sides together and long raw edges aligned, pin the rows together carefully, matching the seams; stitch. Press seams toward the sashing and cornerstone rows.

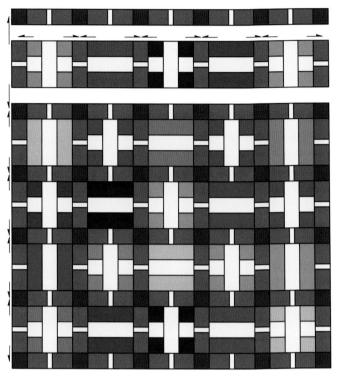

Assembly Diagram

Finishing

Refer to "Finishing Your Project" on pages 26–29 for guidance as needed.

1. Select a quilting design and mark the quilt top as necessary.

2. Center the quilt top and batting over the backing; pin or thread-baste.

3. Hand or machine quilt as desired.

4. Trim the batting and backing as instructed in "Binding and Labeling" on page 27. Use the ⅜ yard of blue print to cut a total of 145" of 2¾"-wide bias binding strips. Use the strips to construct a double-fold bias binding (to finish ½" wide). Sew the binding to the quilt.

5. Make a label and attach it to your quilt.

Nineties Quilt Memories

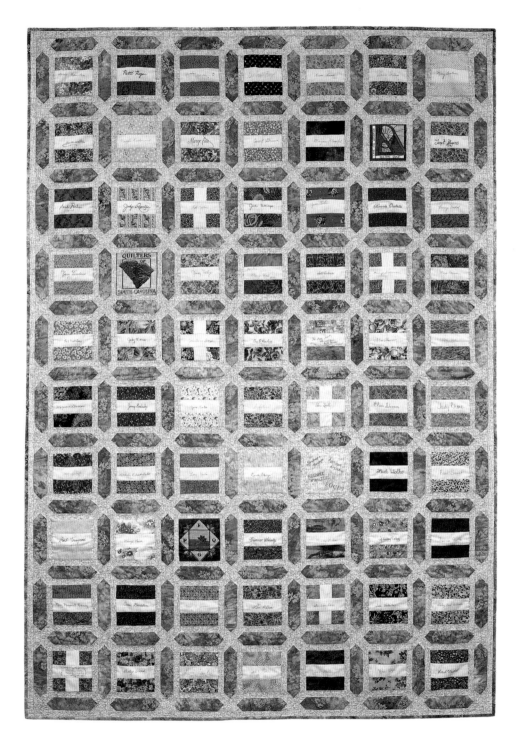

By Ann C. Hawkins, 1999, Seneca, South Carolina, 56¼" x 78¾".

Ann's subtle and sophisticated theme fabric, combined with the architectural structure of her pattern, evoke the cool serenity of Italian palaces. Ann added some special squares to commemorate her guild connections.

Ann Hawkins's answer to our guild's millennium challenge drew delighted gasps from the people who attended our exhibit in 1999. Her soft color palette, combined with sophisticated sashing, created a truly elegant piece. It continues to amaze me that, given the same simple blocks to work with, so many beautiful and unique results are possible.

Ann used the exchange blocks from our guild members, asked good friends to add more to her collection, and made four special squares herself. Three of these squares included photo transfers of quilt-organization logos; the other square held the names of our nearby quilt shop, Heirlooms and Comforts; our FOCUS: Fabric Art group; and two bees that Ann attends regularly. So this is a true memory piece, honoring her quilt friends and clubs here in South Carolina.

Materials

Yardage based on 42"-wide fabric unless otherwise stated.

⅞ yd. muslin or other light fabric for signature strips and special squares

1⅛ yds. *total* of assorted medium print scraps for blocks

3⅛ yds. cream print for framing, sashing, cornerstones, and border

2 yds. seafoam green print for sashing and binding

3½ yds. fabric for backing

60" x 83" piece of batting

Cutting

All measurements include ¼"-wide seam allowances.

From the muslin or other light (signature) fabric, cut:

- 66 rectangles, each 2" x 5", for Rail Fence and Nine Patch Variation blocks

- 6 rectangles, each 2" x 4", for Nine Patch Variation blocks

- 4 squares, each 5" x 5", for special photo or signature squares

From the assorted medium print scraps, cut a *total* of:

- 120 rectangles, each 2" x 5", for Rail Fence blocks

- 12 rectangles, each 2" x 4", for Nine Patch Variation blocks

From the cream print, cut:

- 140 strips, each 1¼" x 5", for framing

- 140 strips, each 1¼" x 6½", for framing

- 628 squares, each 1¼" x 1¼", for sashing

- 88 squares, each 2" x 2", for cornerstones

- 7 strips, each 1¼" x 42", for border

From the seafoam green print, cut:

- 157 rectangles, each 2" x 6½", for sashing

Making the Blocks

1. Refer to Method Two for "Rail Fence Blocks" on page 10. Use 60 muslin or other light 2" x 5" rectangles and the 120 medium print 2" x 5" rectangles to make a total of 60 Rail Fence blocks.

Make 60.

2. Refer to Method Two for "Nine Patch Variation Blocks" on page 11. Use the remaining 6 muslin or other light 2" x 5" rectangles, the 6 muslin or other light 2" x 4" rectangles, and the 12 assorted medium print 2" x 4" rectangles to make a total of 6 Nine Patch Variation blocks.

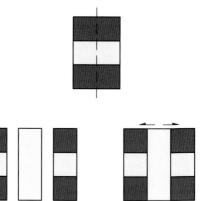

Make 6.

Adding the Lettering and Photo Transfers

1. Refer to "Writing on the Blocks" on page 16. Prepare each block for signature by pressing an appropriately sized strip of freezer paper to the reverse side of the signature area.

2. Distribute the blocks for signatures. When the blocks are returned to you, refer to "Artistic Lettering" on page 16 and augment the signatures as desired. Heat-set the ink as described on page 19.

3. If desired, use the 4 muslin or other light 5" squares and photo-transfer techniques to create 4 special blocks for your quilt. Refer to *Quilting More Memories* by Sandy Bonsib (Martingale & Company, 2001) for comprehensive information on photo-transfer techniques.

   Alternatively, write in these 5" blocks the names of organizations or other key information associated with the friends signing the quilt.

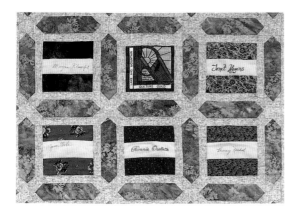

Assembling the Quilt Top

1. Sew a 1¼" x 5" cream print strip to opposite sides of each block. Press seams toward the cream print strips. Repeat to sew a 1¼" x 6½" cream print strip to the top and bottom of each block; press.

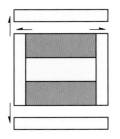

2. Use a mechanical pencil to draw a light diagonal line from corner to corner on the wrong side of each 1¼" cream print square.

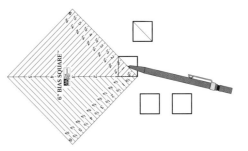

3. Place a marked square right sides together with both left corners of each 2" x 6½" seafoam green strip as shown. Sew directly on the marked lines. Trim the excess fabric, leaving a ¼"-wide seam allowance. Press seams toward the corner triangles.

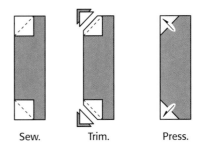

Sew.   Trim.   Press.

4. Repeat step 3 to add a 1¼" cream print square to both right corners of each unit from step 3; press. Make a total of 157 pieced sashing units.

Make 157.

5. Refer to "Arranging Your Blocks" on page 20. Lay out the framed blocks and pieced sashing units in 10 horizontal rows, alternating 8 sashing units and 7 blocks in each row as shown in the assembly diagram on page 40. Refer to the quilt photo on page 37 for additional guidance as necessary.

6. Sew the blocks and sashing units together into horizontal rows. Press seams toward the sashing units.

7. Arrange and sew 8 cream print 2" squares (cornerstones) and 7 sashing units in a horizontal row as shown. Press seams toward the sashing units. Make 11 rows.

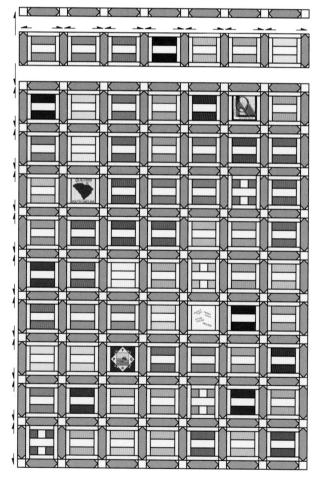

Make 11.

8. Lay out the rows from steps 6 and 7, alternating them as shown in the assembly diagram. With right sides together and long, raw edges aligned, pin the rows together carefully, matching the seams; stitch. Press seams toward the sashing and cornerstone rows.

Assembly Diagram

9. Join the 1¼" x 42" cream print border strips end to end to make a continuous 1¼"-wide strip. Measure the quilt through its horizontal center, and cut 2 border strips to this measurement from the 1¼"-wide strip. Mark the center of the quilt edges and the border strips. With right sides together and long, raw edges aligned, pin the trimmed borders to the top and bottom of the quilt top, matching the center marks and ends and easing as necessary. Press seams toward the borders.

10. Measure the quilt through its vertical center, including the borders you've just added. Cut 2 border strips to this measurement from the remaining 1¼"-wide strip. Follow the procedure described in step 9 to add these borders to the left and right sides of the quilt; press.

Finishing

Refer to "Finishing Your Project" on pages 26–29 for guidance as needed.

1. Select a quilting design and mark the quilt top as necessary.

2. Divide the backing fabric crosswise into 2 equal panels of approximately 63" each. Remove the selvages and join the panels to make a single, large backing panel.

3. Center the quilt top and batting over the backing. The backing seam should run parallel to the top and bottom edges of the quilt top. Pin or thread-baste.

4. Hand or machine quilt as desired.

5. Trim the batting and backing as instructed in "Binding and Labeling" on page 27. Use the remaining seafoam green print to cut a total of 285" of 2¼"-wide bias binding strips. Use the strips to construct a double-fold bias binding (to finish ⅜" wide). Sew the binding to the quilt.

6. Make a label and attach it to your quilt.

Mother Goose and Friends

By Marge Edie, 1999, Clemson, South Carolina, 24" x 30".

Who says that only real people get to sign one of these projects? This piece is perfect for a child's room, with its bright crayon colors and whimsical lettering. Notice that there are intense rainbow hues and also their pastel versions, and the two color groupings work well together.

When I started wondering which groups might sign my quilts, I decided to use imaginary characters—and who better than the heroes and heroines of nursery rhymes? The fun part was designing lettering to match the characters. Mother Goose herself is in charge of all the others, in a motherly way. Wee Willie Winkie is rather shy, Lucy Locket is quite feminine, Old King Cole is regal, and Humpty Dumpty is clumsy.

As you write these names on your quilt, you may find it challenging to keep the length and thickness of the lines and strokes uniform. Varying the color and thickness of the lines helps to disguise imperfections. You can also fix slight imperfections by reworking the lettering until you get consistency. That's how "Little Jack Horner" became so thick!

I hope you can't tell in the photo, but the red ink in "Old King Cole" bled a bit with heat-setting, resulting in a slight aura of pink around that lettering. But I wasn't about to do that hard work over again! This is a great example of why you should test your pens thoroughly before selecting the ones to use in your project.

Materials

Yardage based on 42"-wide fabric unless otherwise stated.

¼ yd. white-on-white print for signature strips

¼ yd. *total* of assorted medium pastel print scraps for blocks

¼ yd. *each* of 9 different brightly colored prints (old gold, orange, red-orange, red, red-violet, magenta, deep turquoise, dark blue, and green) for 60°-triangle blocks, sashing, and border

⅜ yd. multicolored print for 60°-triangle blocks and cornerstones

1 yd. fabric for backing

⅜ yd. forest green print for binding

28" x 34" piece of batting

Cutting

All measurements include ¼"-wide seam allowances.

From the white-on-white print, cut:
- 12 rectangles, each 2" x 5", for Nine Patch Variation and Rail Fence blocks
- 6 rectangles, each 2" x 4", for Nine Patch Variation blocks

From the assorted medium pastel print scraps, cut a *total* of:
- 12 rectangles, each 2" x 5", for Rail Fence blocks
- 12 rectangles, each 2" x 4", for Nine Patch Variation blocks

From the old gold print, cut:
- 5 squares, each 3½" x 3½", for 60°-triangle blocks
- 4 squares, each 2" x 2", for sashing
- 2 rectangles, each 2" x 5", for border

From the orange print, cut:
- 4 squares, each 3½" x 3½", for 60°-triangle blocks
- 3 squares, each 2" x 2", for sashing
- 2 rectangles, each 2" x 5", for border

From the red-orange print, cut:
- 5 squares, each 3½" x 3½", for 60°-triangle blocks
- 5 squares, each 2" x 2", for sashing and border
- 1 rectangle, 2" x 5", for border

From the red print, cut:
- 3 squares, each 3½" x 3½", for 60°-triangle blocks
- 3 squares, each 2" x 2", for sashing and border
- 1 rectangle, 2" x 5", for border

From the red-violet print, cut:
- 5 squares, each 3½" x 3½", for 60°-triangle blocks
- 5 squares, each 2" x 2", for sashing and border
- 1 rectangle, 2" x 5", for border

From the magenta print, cut:
- 5 squares, each 3½" x 3½", for 60°-triangle blocks
- 5 squares, each 2" x 2", for sashing and order
- 1 rectangle, 2" x 5", for border

From the deep turquoise print, cut:
- 4 squares, each 3½" x 3½", for 60°-triangle blocks
- 3 squares, each 2" x 2", for sashing
- 2 rectangles, each 2" x 5", for border

From the dark blue print, cut:
- 5 squares, each 3½" x 3½", for 60°-triangle blocks
- 4 squares, each 2" x 2", for sashing
- 2 rectangles, each 2" x 5", for border

From the green print, cut:
- 4 squares, each 3½" x 3½", for 60°-triangle blocks
- 3 squares, each 2" x 2", for sashing
- 2 rectangles, each 2" x 5", for border

From the multicolored print, cut:
- 100 squares, each 2" x 2", for 60°-triangle blocks and cornerstones

Making the Blocks

1. Refer to Method Two for "Rail Fence Blocks" on page 10. Use 6 white-on-white 2" x 5" rectangles and the 12 assorted medium pastel 2" x 5" rectangles to make a total of 6 Rail Fence blocks.

Make 6.

2. Refer to Method Two for "Nine Patch Variation Blocks" on page 11. Use the remaining 6 white-on-white 2" x 5" rectangles, the 6 white-on-white 2" x 4" rectangles, and the 12 assorted medium pastel 2" x 4" rectangles to make a total of 6 Nine Patch Variation blocks.

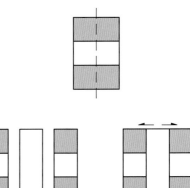

Make 6.

Adding the Lettering

1. Refer to "Writing on the Blocks" on page 16. Prepare each block for signature by pressing an appropriately sized strip of freezer paper to the reverse side of the signature area.

2. Refer to "Artistic Lettering" on page 16, and letter the blocks as desired. If you are making a friendship quilt, distribute the blocks for signatures. When the blocks are returned to you, augment the signatures as desired. Heat-set the ink as described on page 19.

Assembling the Quilt Top

1. Cut each of the 40 assorted brightly colored 3½" squares in half to make a total of 80 rectangles, each 1¾" x 3½". Cut the 2 rectangles resulting from each square in half on opposite diagonals as shown to make a total of 160 "skinny" triangles.

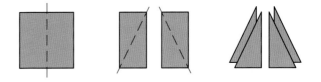

2. Refer to "60°-Triangle Blocks" on page 23. Use 62 multicolored 2" squares and 124 "skinny" triangles from step 1 to make 62 blocks in the color combinations shown.

Make 8
old gold.

Make 6
orange.

Make 8
red-orange.

Make 4
red.

Make 6
green.

Make 8
red-violet.

Make 8
magenta.

Make 6
deep turquoise.

Make 8
dark blue.

3. Sew a 2" brightly colored square between two 60°-triangle blocks, matching the square color to the "skinny" triangles. Press seams away from the triangle squares. Make 31 sashing units.

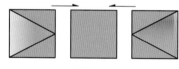

Make 31.

4. Sew 4 sashing units, 2 Rail Fence blocks, and 1 Nine Patch Variation block in a row, referring to the photo on page 41 for color placement. Press seams toward the blocks. Make 2 rows.

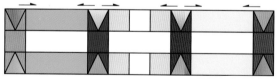

Make 2.

5. Sew 4 sashing units, 1 Rail Fence block, and 2 Nine Patch Variation blocks in a row, referring to the photo on page 41 for color placement. Press seams toward the blocks. Make 2 rows.

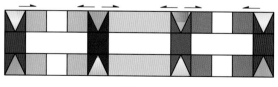

Make 2.

6. Arrange 20 multicolored 2" squares and the remaining sashing units in 5 rows as shown. Each row includes 4 squares and 3 sashing units. Sew the squares and sashing units together. Press seams away from the sashing units.

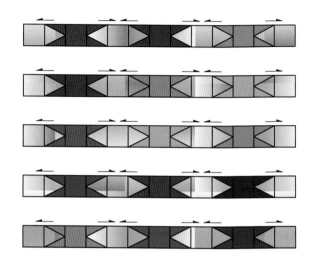

7. Lay out the rows, positioning them by sashing color as shown. With right sides together and long, raw edges aligned, pin the rows together, matching seams; stitch. Press seams toward the block rows.

8. Arrange the 14 assorted brightly colored 2" x 5" rectangles to make 4 border units as shown below. Leave space for the 60°-triangle units. You'll make those in the next step.

9. Use the remaining 36 brightly colored "skinny" triangles and the remaining 2" multicolored squares to make eighteen 60°-triangle blocks. Be sure the "skinny" triangles match the color of the adjacent 2" x 5" brightly colored rectangles, noting that the "skinny" triangle on each side of the triangle block is a different color.

10. Position each new 60°-triangle block in the appropriate border as shown below. Finish each end of the left and right border units with a 2" brightly colored square in the color shown. Sew the squares, triangle squares, and rectangles together to make the 4 border units. Press seams toward the rectangles on the top and bottom border units. Press seams toward the triangle squares on the right and left border units.

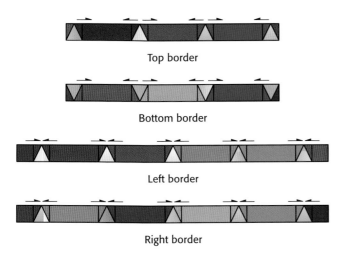

Top border

Bottom border

Left border

Right border

11. With right sides together and long, raw edges aligned, pin the top and bottom border units carefully to the quilt as shown in the diagram at right, matching the seams; stitch. Press seams toward the border units.

12. Repeat step 11 to sew the side border units to the quilt as shown; press.

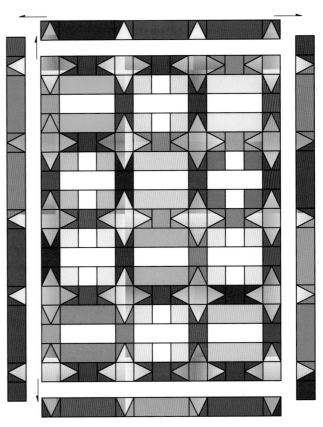

Finishing

Refer to "Finishing Your Project" on pages 26–29 for guidance as needed.

1. Select a quilting design and mark the quilt top as necessary.

2. Center the quilt top and batting over the backing; pin or thread-baste.

3. Hand or machine quilt as desired.

4. Trim the batting and backing as instructed in "Binding and Labeling" on page 27. Use the ⅜ yard of forest green print to cut a total of 120" of 3¾"-wide bias binding strips. Use the strips to construct a double-fold bias binding (to finish ¾" wide). Sew the binding to the quilt.

5. Make a label and attach it to your quilt.

Quilting Friends

By Eleanor Schultz, 1999, Anderson, South Carolina, 56¾" x 69½".

Eleanor's color sense is remarkable and the outcome is a wonderful, cohesive scrap approach. Her background is a perfect contrast to the rich tones of the triangles, and all fabric choices work well to augment the exchange blocks.

Eleanor Schultz's response to our guild's millennium challenge showcases her exceptional talent for the scrap-quilt approach. We are always in awe of her flair for combining a wide variety of colors, textures, and prints to create a perfect visual palette. Your color combinations should be true to your own instincts, but just looking at Eleanor's selection is an education in itself.

Notice that some of Eleanor's light Nine Patch Variation and Rail Fence blocks are surrounded with dark triangles, and some of her dark Nine Patch and Rail Fence blocks are combined with light triangles. In other squares, the values almost match.

Compare this quilt with Ilse Perea's "Almost Amish," below, which uses only one sashing and cornerstone strip between the blocks. Even such a small difference in setting can create quite a different look.

The crisp geometry of this quilt is very easy to accomplish and creates a jewel-like effect of sparkling motifs floating on a subtle background. Even with its generous size, this quilt goes together rather quickly.

Almost Amish by Ilse Perea, 2000, Greenville, South Carolina, 60" x 72".

Materials

Yardage based on 42"-wide fabric unless otherwise stated.

½ yd. muslin or other light fabric for signature strips and title block

⅝ yd. *total* of assorted print scraps for blocks

One 8" x 10" scrap *each* of 32 assorted print and solid-color fabrics for block triangles and cornerstones

2⅛ yds. light print for sashing and setting triangles

1⅛ yds. dark green print for border and binding

3½ yds. fabric for backing

61" x 74" piece of batting

Cutting

All measurements include ¼"-wide seam allowances.

From the muslin or other light (signature) fabric, cut:

- 31 rectangles, each 2" x 5", for Rail Fence and Nine Patch Variation blocks

- 7 rectangles, each 2" x 4", for Nine Patch Variation blocks

- 1 square, 5" x 5", for title block

From the assorted print scraps, cut a *total* of:

- 48 rectangles, each 2" x 5", for Rail Fence blocks

- 14 rectangles, each 2" x 4, for Nine Patch Variation blocks

From *each* 8" x 10" scrap of assorted print and solid-color fabric, cut:

- 2 squares, each 4¼" x 4¼"; cut each square once diagonally to make 2 block triangles (128 total)

- 4 squares, each 2" x 2", for cornerstones

From the light print, cut:

- 128 strips, each 2" x 6⅞", for sashing

- 4 squares, each 14¼" x 14¼"; cut each square twice diagonally to make 4 side setting triangles (16 total)*

- 2 squares, each 7⅜" x 7⅜"; cut each square once diagonally to make 2 corner setting triangles (4 total)

From the dark green print, cut:

- 6 strips, each 2½" x 42", for border

You'll have 2 triangles left over. Set these aside for another project.

Making the Blocks

1. Refer to Method Two for "Rail Fence Blocks" on page 10. Use 24 muslin or other light 2" x 5" rectangles and the 48 assorted print 2" x 5" rectangles to make a total of 24 Rail Fence blocks.

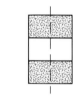

Make 24.

2. Refer to Method Two for "Nine Patch Variation Blocks" on page 11. Use the remaining 7 muslin or other light 2" x 5" rectangles, the 7 muslin or other light 2" x 4" rectangles, and the 14 assorted print 2" x 4" rectangles to make a total of 7 Nine Patch Variation blocks.

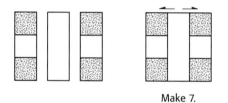

Make 7.

Adding the Lettering

1. Refer to "Writing on the Blocks" on page 16. Prepare each block for signature by pressing an appropriately sized strip of freezer paper to the reverse side of the signature area.

2. Distribute the blocks for signatures. When the blocks are returned to you, refer to "Artistic Lettering" on page 16 and augment the signatures as desired. Heat-set the ink as described on page 19.

3. Use the 5" muslin or other light square to create a special title block for your quilt.

Assembling the Quilt Top

1. Sew a matching print or solid-color block triangle to opposite sides of each Rail Fence block. Press seams toward the triangles. Repeat to sew a matching print or solid-color block triangle to the remaining sides of each block; press. Trim the squares to measure 6⅞" x 6⅞".

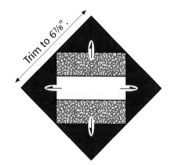

2. Repeat step 1 to sew matching print or solid-color triangles to all sides of each Nine Patch Variation block and all sides of the 5" title block; press and trim.

3. Sew each unit from steps 1 and 2 between 2 light print 2" x 6⅞" sashing strips. Press seams toward the sashing strips.

4. Sew each remaining 2" x 6⅞" light print strip between 2 matching 2" squares of print or solid-color fabric. Press seams toward the sashing strips. You'll have 32 pairs of matching sashing units.

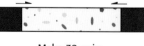

Make 32 pairs.

5. Sew each unit from step 3 between 2 matching sashing units from step 4. Press seams toward the sashing units.

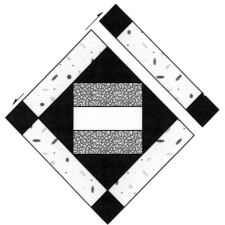

6. Refer to "Arranging Your Blocks" on page 20. Lay out the sashed blocks, the side setting triangles, and the corner setting triangles in diagonal rows as shown in the assembly diagram below. Refer to the quilt photo on page 46 for additional guidance as necessary.

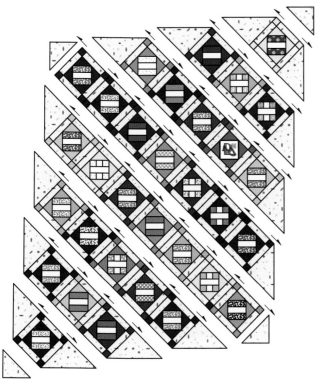

Assembly Diagram

7. Sew the blocks and side setting triangles together to make 8 diagonal rows. Press seams as shown in the assembly diagram.

8. With right sides together and long, raw edges aligned, pin the rows together carefully, matching seams; stitch. Press as desired. Add corner setting triangles to complete the quilt center; press. Square up the quilt top as necessary, making sure to leave a ¼"-wide seam allowance all around the outside edge.

9. Join the 2½" x 42" dark green print border strips end to end to make a continuous 2½"-wide strip. Measure the quilt through its horizontal center, and cut 2 border strips to this measurement from the 2½"-wide strip. Mark the center of the quilt edges and the border strips. With right sides together and long, raw edges aligned, pin the trimmed borders to the top and bottom of the quilt top, matching the center marks and ends and easing as necessary. Press seams toward the borders.

10. Measure the quilt through its vertical center, including the borders you've just added. Cut 2 border strips to this measurement from the remaining 2½"-wide strip. Follow the procedure described in step 9 to add these borders to the left and right sides of the quilt; press.

Finishing

Refer to "Finishing Your Project" on pages 26–29 for guidance as needed.

1. Select a quilting design and mark the quilt top as necessary.

2. Divide the backing fabric crosswise into 2 equal panels of approximately 63" each. Remove the selvages and join the panels to make a single, large backing panel.

3. Center the quilt top and batting over the backing. The backing seam should run parallel to the top and bottom edges of the quilt top. Pin or thread-baste.

4. Hand or machine quilt as desired.

5. Trim the batting and backing as instructed in "Binding and Labeling" on page 27. Use the remaining dark green print to cut a total of 265" of 2¾"-wide bias binding strips. Use the strips to construct a double-fold bias binding (to finish ½" wide). Sew the binding to the quilt.

6. Make a label and attach it to your quilt.

Mosaic

By Marge Edie, 1999, Clemson, South Carolina, 20½" x 32½".

I had fun selecting these brown-toned blacks and the corresponding grays and beiges. Try to imagine this quilt without the red-orange cornerstones; they bring vitality to an otherwise somber piece.

I pieced this small quilt and showed it to my FOCUS art quilt group. They all felt it looked like a mosaic tile design, hence the name. Pat Kilburg said it reminded her of the words of an old traditional song, "I Dreamt I Dwelt in Marble Halls," so I researched the lyrics with the idea of writing them on the blocks. However, they didn't fit the completed top, so I had to compose my own poem!

I wrote out the words in red, thickened the vertical strokes, and lightly shaded the lower portions with black. Manipulations such as shading help camouflage any imperfections.

When I had completed the lettering, I used an iron to heat-set the ink, but some steam still in my iron caused the ink to run. I had to carefully "unpick" some of the signature segments, replace them, and rewrite the ruined portions of the poem. Important lessons were learned here: test your pens before committing to them, and do your lettering on the blocks before sewing them together.

Materials

Yardage based on 42"-wide fabric unless otherwise stated.

⅜ yd. *total* of assorted beige print scraps for signature strips and sashing

⅓ yd. *total* of assorted medium gray print scraps for blocks

½ yd. *total* of assorted black print scraps for sashing

¼ yd. red-orange print for cornerstones

1 yd. fabric for backing

¼ yd. black print for binding

25" x 37" piece of batting

Cutting

All measurements include ¼"-wide seam allowances.

From the assorted beige print scraps, cut a *total* of:

- 15 rectangles, each 2" x 5", for Rail Fence and Nine Patch Variation blocks

- 7 rectangles, each 2" x 4", for Nine Patch Variation blocks

- 19 squares, each 2¾" x 2¾", for quarter-square-triangle blocks

From the assorted medium gray print scraps, cut a *total* of:

- 16 rectangles, each 2" x 5", for Rail Fence blocks

- 14 rectangles, each 2" x 4", for Nine Patch Variation blocks

From the assorted black print scraps, cut a *total* of:

- 19 squares, each 2¾" x 2¾", for quarter-square-triangle blocks

- 76 squares, each 2" x 2", for sashing

From the red-orange print, cut:

- 24 squares, each 2" x 2", for cornerstones

Making the Blocks

1. Refer to Method Two for "Rail Fence Blocks" on page 10. Use 8 assorted beige 2" x 5" rectangles and the 16 assorted medium gray 2" x 5" rectangles to make a total of 8 Rail Fence blocks.

Make 8.

2. Refer to Method Two for "Nine Patch Variation Blocks" on page 11. Use the remaining 7 assorted beige 2" x 5" rectangles, the 7 assorted beige 2" x 4" rectangles, and the 14 assorted medium gray 2" x 4" rectangles to make a total of 7 Nine Patch Variation blocks.

Make 7.

Adding the Lettering

1. Refer to "Writing on the Blocks" on page 16. Prepare each block for lettering by pressing an appropriately sized strip of freezer paper to the reverse side of the signature area.

2. Refer to "Artistic Lettering" on page 16, and letter the blocks as desired. If you are making a friendship quilt, distribute the blocks for signatures. When the blocks are returned to you, augment the signatures as desired. Heat-set the ink as described on page 19.

Assembling the Quilt Top

1. Refer to "Quarter-Square-Triangle Blocks" on page 21. Pair a 2¾" beige print square and a 2¾" black print square to make a quarter-square-triangle block. Make 38 blocks in a variety of beige and black fabric combinations.

Make 38.

2. Sew a quarter-square-triangle block from step 1 between 2 assorted black 2" squares to make a sashing unit. Press seams toward the black squares. Make 38.

Make 38.

3. Refer to "Arranging Your Blocks" on page 20. Arrange 4 sashing units from step 2, 2 Rail Fence blocks, and 1 Nine Patch Variation block in a horizontal row as shown. Sew the sashing units and blocks together. Press seams toward the sashing units. Make 3 rows.

Make 3.

4. Arrange 4 sashing units from step 2, 1 Rail Fence block, and 2 Nine Patch Variation blocks in a horizontal row as shown. Sew the sashing units and blocks together. Press seams toward the sashing units. Make 2 rows.

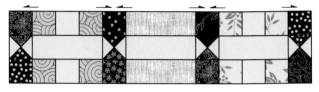

Make 2.

5. Arrange and sew 4 red-orange 2" squares and 3 sashing units in a horizontal row as shown. Press seams toward the sashing units. Make 6 rows.

Make 6.

6. Lay out the rows from steps 3 through 5, alternating them as shown in the quilt photo on page 50. With right sides together and long, raw edges aligned, pin the rows together carefully, matching the seams; stitch. Press seams toward the sashing rows.

Finishing

Refer to "Finishing Your Project" on pages 26–29 for guidance as needed.

1. Select a quilting design and mark the quilt top as necessary.

2. Center the quilt top and batting over the backing; pin or thread-baste.

3. Hand or machine quilt as desired.

4. Trim the batting and backing as instructed in "Binding and Labeling" on page 27. Use the ¼ yard of black print to cut a total of 120" of 2¾"-wide bias binding strips. Use the strips to construct a double-fold bias binding (to finish ½" wide). Sew the binding to the quilt.

5. Make a label and attach it to your quilt.

FOCUS

By Marge Edie, 2001, Clemson, South Carolina, 29½" x 36½".

If I weren't careful, all of my quilts would be in shades of peach. Because I love this range of colors so much, I had my cohorts in our FOCUS: Fabric Art group sign these squares.

This quilt gave me the opportunity to make use of some really vibrant bits and pieces in my stash, and I loved working with such lively colors. Notice that I chose slightly darker shades of the various fabrics to use in the outer rectangles and squares of the Nine Patch Variation and Rail Fence blocks around the perimeter of the quilt. This results in the illusion of a border without the work of actually adding one.

Making lots of little quarter-square-triangle blocks is rather time-consuming, but I think the end result is worth it—they add such sparkle to the quilt! I had my best quilt friends—members of our FOCUS: Art Quilt group—sign the squares. The signature areas were created from a piece of Mickey Lawler's "Skydyes" fabric that has a little opalescence on the surface, making it even more beautiful. The black fabric was also purchased through Mickey's company, and some of the rust and medium rusts were hand-dyed by Marjan Kluepfel, a member of FOCUS. I like the way the design showcases these gorgeous fabrics.

Materials

Yardage based on 42"-wide fabric unless otherwise stated.
¼ yd. light peach print for signature strips
¼ yd. medium rust print for signature strips
¾ yd. *total* of assorted richly colored (e.g., magenta, lilac, rust, coral, orchid, purple, and rose) prints for blocks and sashing
¼ yd. magenta-purple print for sashing
⅝ yd. black print for sashing and binding
¼ yd. coral print for sashing
⅛ yd. purple print for cornerstones
1⅛ yds. fabric for backing
34" x 40" piece of batting

Cutting

All measurements include ¼"-wide seam allowances.

From the light peach print, cut:
- 4 rectangles, each 2" x 5", for Rail Fence and Nine Patch Variation blocks
- 2 rectangles, each 2" x 4", for Nine Patch Variation blocks
- 4 squares, each 5" x 5", for Snowball blocks

From the medium rust print, cut:
- 18 rectangles, each 2" x 5", for Rail Fence and Nine Patch Variation blocks
- 4 rectangles, each 2" x 4", for Nine Patch Variation blocks

From the assorted richly colored prints, cut a *total* of:
- 32 rectangles, each 2" x 5", for Rail Fence blocks
- 12 rectangles, each 2" x 4", for Nine Patch Variation blocks
- 16 squares, each 2" x 2", for Snowball blocks
- 40 squares, each 2¾" x 2¾", for quarter-square-triangle blocks*

From the magenta-purple print, cut:
- 25 squares, each 2¾" x 2¾", for quarter-square- and combination-square-triangle blocks

From the black print, cut:
- 25 squares, each 2¾" x 2¾", for quarter-square- and combination-square-triangle blocks
- 10 squares, each 2⅜" x 2⅜", for combination-square-triangle blocks

From the coral print, cut:
- 49 squares, each 2" x 2", for sashing

From the purple print, cut:
- 20 squares, each 2" x 2", for cornerstones

*Cut these squares in matching pairs.

Cutting for the Diagonal Strip Blocks

In addition to cutting the strips indicated in the instructions on the previous page, you'll need to cut the following strips for the Diagonal Strip blocks. To make the most economical use of fabric, cut the strips on the straight grain of the fabric, referring to Method Two for "Diagonal Strip Blocks" on page 14.

Fabric	Total No. of Strips	Strip Width	Strip Length
Light peach print	2	1⁹⁄₁₆"	21"
Assorted richly colored prints	4	1⁹⁄₁₆"	21"

Making the Blocks

1. Refer to Method Two for "Rail Fence Blocks" on page 10. Use 2 light peach 2" x 5" rectangles and 4 assorted richly colored 2" x 5" rectangles to make a total of 2 Rail Fence blocks.

Make 2.

2. Repeat step 1, using 14 medium rust 2" x 5" rectangles and 28 assorted richly colored 2" x 5" rectangles to make an additional 14 Rail Fence blocks. These blocks will be used to construct the quilt border.

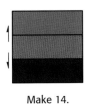

Make 14.

3. Refer to Method Two for "Nine Patch Variation Blocks" on page 11. Use 2 light peach 2" x 5" rectangles, the 2 light peach 2" x 4" rectangles, and 4 assorted richly colored 2" x 4" rectangles to make a total of 2 Nine Patch Variation blocks.

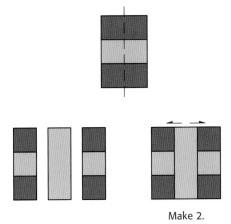

Make 2.

4. Repeat step 3, using 4 medium rust 2" x 5" rectangles, the 4 medium rust 2" x 4" print rectangles, and 8 assorted richly colored 2" x 4" rectangles to make 4 more Nine Patch Variation blocks. These blocks will be used as the corner blocks in the quilt border.

Make 4.

5. Refer to Method Two for "Snowball Blocks" on page 12. Use the 4 light peach 5" squares and the 16 assorted richly colored 2" squares to make 4 Snowball blocks.

Make 4.

6. Refer to Method Two for "Diagonal Strip Blocks" on page 14. Use the 2 light peach 1⁹⁄₁₆" x 21" strips and the 4 assorted richly colored 1⁹⁄₁₆" x 21" strips to make a total of 2 strip sets.

Make 2.

7. Sew the strip sets from step 6 together to make a strip-set tube. Use the tube to make a total of 4 Diagonal Strip blocks.

Make 1.

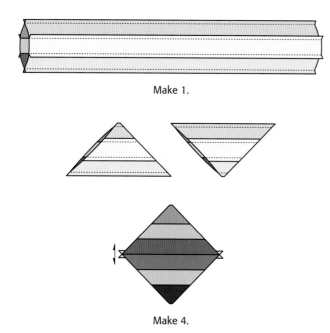

Make 4.

Adding the Lettering

1. Refer to "Writing on the Blocks" on page 16. Prepare each block from "Making the Blocks" (steps 1, 3, 5, and 7) for signature by pressing an appropriately sized strip of freezer paper to the reverse side of the signature area.

2. Distribute the blocks for signatures. When the blocks are returned to you, refer to "Artistic Lettering" on page 16 and augment the signatures as desired. Heat-set the ink as described on page 19.

Assembling the Quilt Top

1. Refer to "Quarter-Square-Triangle Blocks" on page 21. Pair a 2¾" magenta-purple square and a 2¾" richly colored square to make 2 half-square-triangle blocks. (Reserve a matching 2¾" richly colored square for each one used in this step.) Make 40 half-square-triangle blocks.

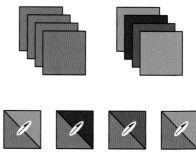

Make 40 total.

2. Pair the reserved, matching 2¾" richly colored square and a 2¾" black square to make 2 half-square-triangle blocks. Make 40.

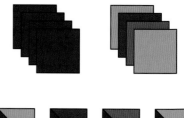

Make 40 total.

3. Pair matching units from steps 1 and 2 to make a total of 80 quarter-square-triangle blocks.

Make 80 total.

4. Refer to "Combination-Square-Triangle Blocks" on page 22. Pair a 2¾" magenta-purple square and a 2¾" black square to make 2 half-square-triangle blocks. Make 10.

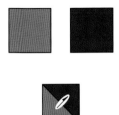

Make 10.

5. Pair each half-square-triangle block from step 4 with a 2⅜" black square to make 4 combination-square-triangle blocks. Make 20; set 2 aside for another project.

Make 20.
Set 2 aside.

6. Refer to the diagram below and the quilt photo on page 53. Arrange the blocks from "Making the Blocks," steps 1, 3, 5, and 7 on pages 55–56, in 4 horizontal rows of 3 blocks each as shown. Leave space for sashing units and cornerstones.

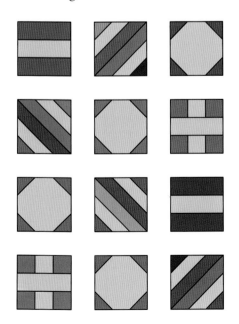

7. Arrange the quarter-square-triangle blocks from step 3 at the corner intersections of the blocks you've arranged in step 6 as shown. Position the triangle blocks carefully, and note that the radiating points of the star-shaped intersections are the same richly colored print.

8. Complete each sashing unit by adding the 2" coral print squares as shown.

9. Assemble the vertical and horizontal sashing units. Work on one sashing unit at a time so you do not lose track of the color sequence. For each sashing unit, sew the 2" coral print square between the 2 adjacent quarter-square-triangle blocks as shown. Press seams toward the coral squares. Replace the unit, and move on to the next until you have completed all 31 sashing units.

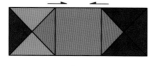

Make 31.

10. Fill in the cornerstones by adding the 20 purple 2" squares. Do not sew the quilt top together yet.

11. Refer to the assembly diagram at right and the quilt photo on page 53. Arrange the remaining Rail Fence blocks around the perimeter of the quilt, and place the Nine Patch Variation blocks in the corners as shown. Leave space for sashing units and cornerstones.

12. For each sashing unit, sew a remaining 2" coral print square between a remaining quarter-square-triangle block and a combination-square-triangle block as shown. Press seams toward the coral squares. Make 18 sashing units.

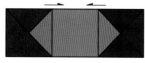

Make 18.

13. Refer to the assembly diagram and the quilt photo. Place the newly assembled sashing units between the Rail Fence and Nine Patch Variation blocks you've arranged in step 11 as shown. Position the combination-square-triangle blocks nearest the outside edge of the quilt, and note that the radiating points of any new star-shaped intersections are the same richly colored print.

14. Sew the blocks and vertical sashing units together to make rows 1, 3, 5, 7, 9, and 11. Press seams toward the sashing units.

15. Sew the horizontal sashing units and the purple print cornerstones together to make rows 2, 4, 6, 8, and 10. Press seams toward the sashing units.

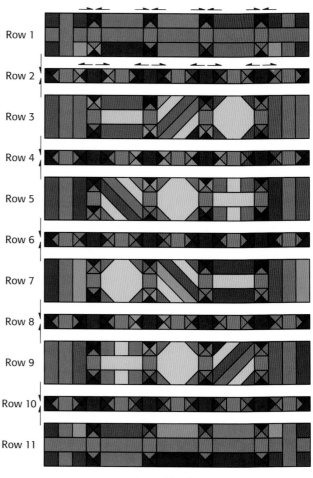

Row 1
Row 2
Row 3
Row 4
Row 5
Row 6
Row 7
Row 8
Row 9
Row 10
Row 11

Assembly Diagram

16. With right sides together and long, raw edges aligned, pin the rows together, matching the seams; stitch. Press seams toward the sashing rows.

Finishing

Refer to "Finishing Your Project" on pages 26–29 for guidance as needed.

1. Select a quilting design and mark the quilt top as necessary.

2. Center the quilt top and batting over the backing; pin or thread-baste.

3. Hand or machine quilt as desired.

4. Trim the batting and backing as instructed in "Binding and Labeling" on page 27. Use the remaining black print to cut a total of 150" of 3¾"-wide bias binding strips. Use the strips to construct a double-fold bias binding (to finish ¾" wide). Sew the binding to the quilt.

5. Make a label and attach it to your quilt.

Wordsmiths

By Marge Edie, 2001, Clemson, South Carolina, 20¼" x 26¼".

Several folks at Martingale & Company were nice enough to sign these squares. I selected fabrics that reminded me of colors and textures found in the libraries of fine old mansions—a fitting environment for these contributors to the world of publishing.

My design instincts move toward very balanced, orderly structures, so it's hard for me to be random. Here I decided to go against my inclinations and use unmatched sashing to add a little "zing" to the quilt. The block arrangement is almost identical to that of "FOCUS" (page 53), but the unpredictable sashing completely changes the feel of the piece. I'll include my sashing-unit choices, but I encourage you to develop your own combinations to suit your own tastes.

Materials

Yardage based on 42"-wide fabric unless otherwise stated.

¼ yd. muslin or other light fabric for signature strips

⅛ yd. *each* of 6 assorted jewel-tone prints for blocks and sashing

⅛ yd. *each* of 3 assorted yellow or gold prints for sashing

½ yd. theme print for sashing

¼ yd. black print for sashing and cornerstones

4 squares, each 2" x 2", of dark blue print for cornerstones

1 yd. fabric for backing

¼ yd. blue print for binding

25" x 31" piece of batting

Cutting

All measurements include ¼"-wide seam allowances.

Use a fine-tip permanent marker to trace the pattern for piece A (page 63) onto a sheet of template plastic. Cut out the template.

From the muslin or other light (signature) fabric, cut:

- 5 rectangles, each 2" x 5", for Rail Fence and Nine Patch Variation blocks

- 3 rectangles, each 2" x 4", for Nine Patch Variation blocks

- 4 squares, each 5" x 5", for Snowball blocks

From the 6 assorted jewel-tone prints, cut a *total* of:

- 4 rectangles, each 2" x 5", for Rail Fence blocks

- 6 rectangles, each 2" x 4", for Nine Patch Variation blocks

- 16 squares, each 2" x 2", for Snowball blocks

- 6 squares, each 2¾" x 2¾", for quarter-square triangle blocks

- 5 squares, each 2⅜" x 2⅜", for half-square triangle blocks

- 2 piece A, for sashing

From the 3 assorted yellow or gold prints, cut a *total* of:

- 9 squares, each 2¾" x 2¾", for quarter-square-triangle blocks

- 8 squares, each 2" x 2", for sashing

From the theme print, cut:

- 17 squares, each 2¾" x 2¾", for quarter-square-triangle blocks

- 13 squares, each 2⅜" x 2⅜", for half-square-triangle blocks

- 45 squares, each 2" x 2", for sashing

- 2 piece A, for sashing

From the black print, cut:

- 6 squares, each 2¾" x 2¾", for quarter-square-triangle blocks

- 2 squares, each 2⅜" x 2⅜", for quarter-square-triangle and half-square-triangle blocks

- 12 squares, each 2" x 2", for cornerstones

Cutting for the Diagonal Strip Blocks

In addition to cutting the strips indicated in the instructions above, you'll need to cut the strips listed in the table on the following page for the Diagonal Strip blocks. To make the most economical use of fabric, cut the strips on the straight grain of the fabric, referring to Method Three for "Diagonal Strip Blocks" on page 15.

Fabric	Total No. of Strips	Strip Width	Strip Length
Muslin or other light (signature) print	6	1⁹⁄₁₆"	8"
Assorted jewel-tone prints	12 (total)	1⁹⁄₁₆"	8"

Making the Blocks

1. Refer to Method Two for "Rail Fence Blocks" on page 10. Use 2 muslin or other light 2" x 5" rectangles and the 4 assorted jewel-tone 2" x 5" rectangles to make a total of 2 Rail Fence blocks.

Make 2.

2. Refer to Method Two for "Nine Patch Variation Blocks" on page 11. Use 3 muslin or other light 2" x 5" rectangles, the 3 muslin or other light 2" x 4" rectangles, and the 6 assorted jewel-tone 2" x 4" rectangles to make a total of 3 Nine Patch Variation blocks.

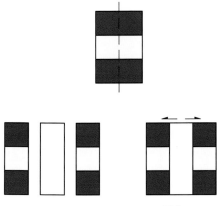

Make 3.

3. Refer to Method Two for "Snowball Blocks" on page 12. Use the 4 muslin or other light 5" squares and the 16 assorted jewel-tone 2" squares to make 4 Snowball blocks.

Make 4.

4. Refer to Method Three for "Diagonal Strip Blocks" on page 15. Use the 6 muslin 1⁹⁄₁₆" x 8" strips and the 12 assorted jewel-tone 1⁹⁄₁₆" x 8" strips to make a total of 3 Diagonal Strip blocks.

Make 3.

Adding the Lettering

1. Refer to "Writing on the Blocks" on page 16. Prepare each block for lettering by pressing an appropriately sized strip of freezer paper to the reverse side of the signature area.

2. Refer to "Artistic Lettering" on page 16, and letter the blocks as desired. If you are making a friendship quilt, distribute the blocks for signatures. When the blocks are returned to you, augment the signatures as desired. Heat-set the ink as described on page 19.

Assembling the Quilt Top

With these instructions, you'll make more triangle-square blocks than you need in steps 1–4. Sometimes this occurs because of the methods used to construct these blocks. However, I've also allowed for a few extras to give you lots of color and fabric combinations as you construct the various sashing units in step 5.

You may find it useful to refer to the assembly diagram on page 63 and the quilt photo on page 59 as you select color combinations for the individual blocks, and to preview the various effects possible as you arrange them into sashing units.

1. Refer to "Quarter-Square-Triangle Blocks" on page 21. Use 4 assorted jewel-tone 2¾" squares, 5 assorted yellow or gold 2¾" squares, 11 theme-print 2¾" squares, and 2 black 2¾" squares to make a total of 22 quarter-square-triangle blocks in a variety of color combinations.

Make 22 total.

2. Refer to "Combination-Square-Triangle Blocks" on page 22. Use 2 assorted jewel-tone 2¾" squares, 4 assorted yellow or gold 2¾" squares, 6 theme-print 2¾" squares, and 4 black 2¾" squares to make a total of 16 half-square-triangle blocks in a variety of color combinations.

Make 16 total.

3. Pair a half-square-triangle block from step 2 with 1 jewel-tone 2⅜" square, 12 theme-print 2⅜" squares, and 1 black 2⅜" square to make a total of 28 combination-square-triangle blocks in a variety of color combinations. You'll have 2 half-square-triangle blocks left over; set them aside for another project.

Make 28 total.
Set 2 aside.

4. Refer to "Half-Square-Triangle Blocks" on page 20. Use 4 assorted jewel-tone 2⅜" squares, 1 theme-print 2⅜" square, and 1 black 2⅜" square to make a total of 6 half-square-triangle blocks.

Make 6 total.

5. Use the 2" assorted yellow or gold squares, the 2" theme-print squares, and various triangle-square blocks from steps 1 and 4 to make a total of 29 sashing units in the combinations shown.

Make 4.

Make 1.

Make 7.

Make 5.

Make 4.

Make 3.

Make 1.

Make 1.

Make 1.

Make 1.

Make 1.

6. Pair a jewel-tone and theme-print A piece to make a sashing unit as shown. Make 2.

Make 2.

7. Refer to the assembly diagram at right. Lay out the blocks, sashing units from steps 5 and 6, the 2" black and blue squares, 2 remaining half-square-triangle blocks, and 2 remaining combination-square-triangle blocks to use as cornerstones. Set the remaining triangle-square blocks aside for another project.

8. Sew the horizontal sashing units and the black, blue, or triangle-square cornerstones together to make rows 1, 3, 5, 7, and 9. Press seams toward the sashing units.

9. Sew the blocks and vertical sashing units together to make rows 2, 4, 6, and 8. Press seams toward the sashing units.

10. With right sides together and long, raw edges aligned, pin the rows together, matching the seams; stitch. Press seams toward the sashing rows.

Finishing

Refer to "Finishing Your Project" on pages 26–29 for guidance as needed.

1. Select a quilting design and mark the quilt top as necessary.
2. Center the quilt top and batting over the backing; pin or thread-baste.
3. Hand or machine quilt as desired.
4. Trim the batting and backing as instructed in "Binding and Labeling" on page 27. Use the blue print to cut a total of 110" of 2¼"-wide bias binding strips. Use the strips to construct a double-fold bias binding (to finish ⅜" wide). Sew the binding to the quilt.
5. Make a label and attach it to your quilt.

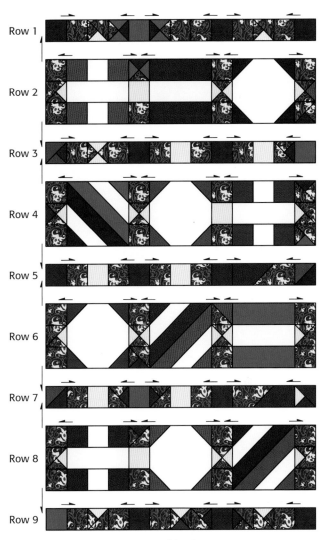

Assembly Diagram

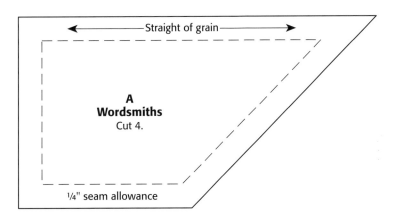

Nauti-Thoughts

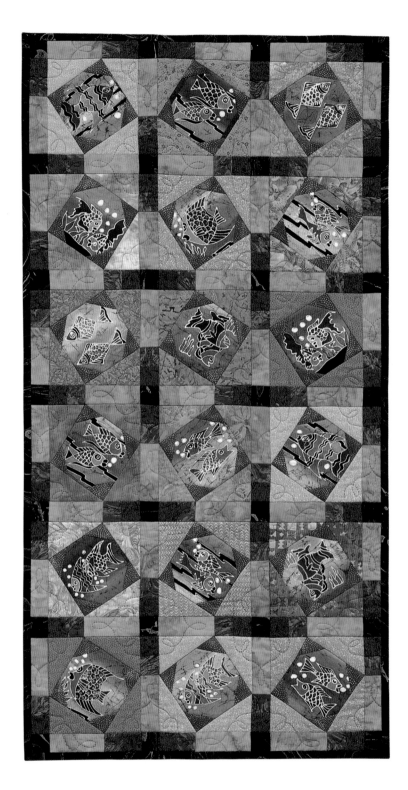

By Marge Edie, 2000, Clemson, South Carolina, 24¾" x 47¼".

I found these cute batik squares in Ellen Simon's shop in Columbia, South Carolina. Marketed by Lee Anne's Batiks, they were the perfect size for this jaunty design.

Because the "flow" of this quilt invokes the ocean and the sashing reminds me of maritime signaling flags, I searched for interesting fabric with a nautical theme. I found these clever batik fish squares and was pleased that they were approximately 5" square. As a result, you will just have to imagine signatures in these blocks, rather than fish, if you wish to use this arrangement in a friendship exchange quilt.

Note that the sashing strips in this quilt, as well as in "Whirling Ribbons" (page 69), are cut ¼" narrower, at 1¾", than the sashing for other quilts in this book. Gale Pemberton's friendship quilt, "Some Jewels in My Life" (below), is a version of "Nauti-Thoughts" without the sashing. She combines lots of pure crayon colors with the softer, less intense hues of the exchange blocks for a very successful, scrappy look.

I enjoyed using several fabrics for the block triangles in "Nauti-Thoughts." Then, to unify the quilt, I used only three fabrics for the sashing, one for the cornerstones, and one for the corners of the Snowball blocks. You may elect a scrappier look by introducing a variety of prints. If you keep your values or shades organized, the geometry will still flow nicely.

If you decide, as I did, to include little "scenes" in your Snowball blocks, remember that the corners will be clipped off a bit. Be sure to select fabric that will not lose important details when the blocks are constructed.

Materials:

Yardage based on 42"-wide fabric unless otherwise stated.
18 squares, each 5" x 5", of theme fabric for blocks
⅜ yd. medium magenta print for blocks
Scraps of 18 assorted coordinating prints for block triangles
¼ yd. dark magenta print for sashing
¼ yd. medium green print for sashing
⅜ yd. bright green print for sashing
⅝ yd. black print for cornerstones and binding
1½ yds. fabric for backing
29" x 52" piece of batting

Cutting

All measurements include ¼"-wide seam allowances.
From the medium magenta print, cut:
• 72 squares, each 2" x 2", for Snowball blocks

From *each* of the 18 coordinating print scraps, cut:
• 2 rectangles, each 3¼" x 4¹³⁄₁₆", for block triangles

From the dark magenta print, cut:
• 2 strips, each 1¾" x 42", for sashing

From the medium green print, cut:
• 2 strips, each 1¾" x 42", for sashing

From the bright green print, cut:
• 2 strips, each 4¼" x 42", for sashing

From the black print, cut:
• 28 squares, each 1¾" x 1¾", for cornerstones

Making the Blocks

1. Refer to Method One for "Snowball Blocks" on page 12. Use the 5" squares of theme fabric and the 72 medium magenta 2" squares to make a total of 18 Snowball blocks.

Sew.

Trim.

Press.
Make 18.

2. Cut matching 3¼" x 4¹³⁄₁₆" rectangles in half on the diagonal from upper left to lower right as shown to make a total of 36 block triangles.

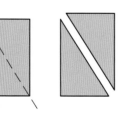

3. Sew a block triangle with a matching coordinating print to opposite sides of a Snowball block. Press seams toward the triangles. Repeat to sew a matching coordinating print block triangle to the remaining sides of the block; press. Make 9 blocks. Each block should measure 6¾" x 6¾".

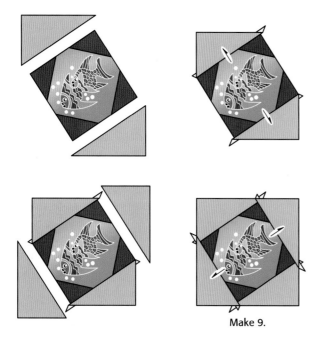

Make 9.

4. Cut the remaining coordinating print 3¼" x 4¹³⁄₁₆" rectangles in half on the diagonal from upper right to lower left as shown to make a total of 36 block triangles. Repeat step 3 to sew 4 matching coordinating block triangles to each remaining Snowball block. Make 9 blocks.

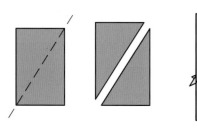

Make 9.

5. Sew a 1¾" x 42" dark magenta strip, a 1¾" x 42" medium green strip, and a 4¼" x 42" bright green strip together as shown to make a strip set that measures 6¾" x 42". Press seams toward the dark magenta strip. Make 2 strip sets.

6. Crosscut the strip sets into a total of 45 segments, each 1¾" wide, to use as sashing units.

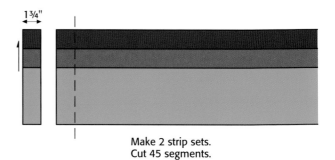

Make 2 strip sets.
Cut 45 segments.

7. Refer to "Arranging Your Blocks" on page 20. Arrange 4 sashing units from step 6, 2 blocks from step 3, and 1 block from step 4 in a horizontal row, making sure blocks and sashing units are positioned as shown. Sew the sashing units and blocks together. Press seams toward the sashing units. Make 3 rows.

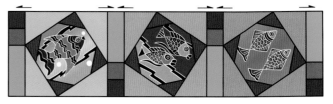

Make 3 rows.

8. Arrange 4 sashing units from step 6, 1 block from step 3, and 2 blocks from step 4 in a horizontal row, making sure blocks and sashing units are positioned as shown. Sew the sashing units and blocks together. Press seams toward the sashing units. Make 3 rows.

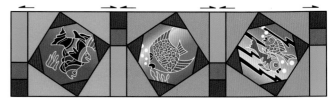

Make 3 rows.

9. Arrange and sew 4 black 1¾" squares and 3 remaining sashing units in a horizontal row, making sure the sashing units are positioned as shown. Press seams toward the sashing units. Make 7 rows.

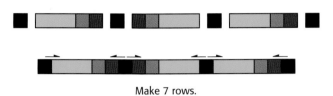

Make 7 rows.

10. Lay out the rows from steps 7–9, alternating them as shown in the assembly diagram at right. With right sides together and long raw edges aligned, pin the rows together, matching the seams; stitch. Press seams toward the sashing rows.

Finishing

Refer to "Finishing Your Project" on pages 26–29 for guidance as needed.

1. Select a quilting design and mark the quilt top as necessary.
2. Center the quilt top and batting over the backing; pin or thread-baste.
3. Hand or machine quilt as desired. You may wish to trace and use the pattern shown on page 68, using a variety of threads to quilt motifs by hand and/or machine.
4. Trim the batting and backing as instructed in "Binding and Labeling" on page 27. Use the remaining black print to cut a total of 160" of 2¾"-wide bias binding strips. Use the strips to construct a double-fold bias binding (to finish ½" wide). Sew the binding to the quilt.
5. Make a label and attach it to your quilt.

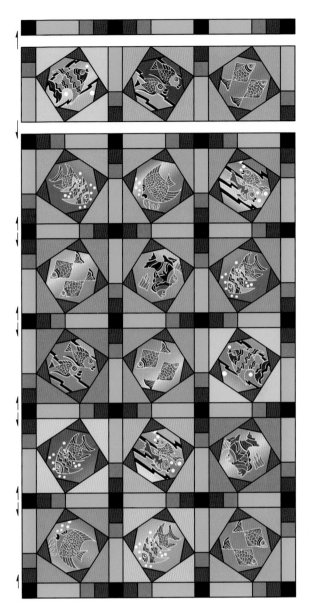

Assembly Diagram

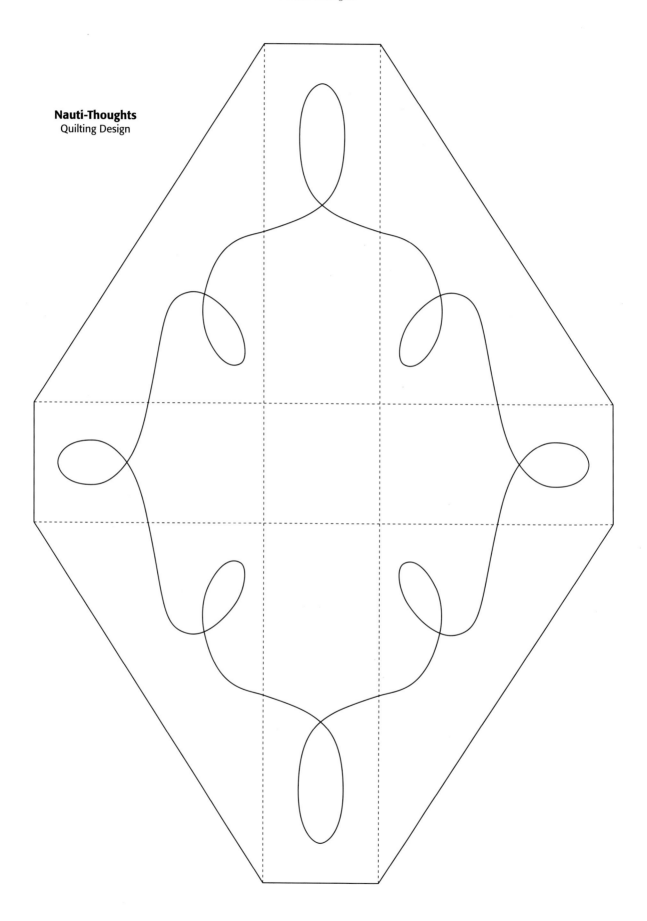

Nauti-Thoughts
Quilting Design

Whirling Ribbons

By Marge Edie, 2001, Clemson, South Carolina, 41⅝" x 57⅞".

My new granddaughter, Alyssa Diana Cooper, owns this quilt, but the sweet baby didn't actually get to hold it until this book went to the printer. The color scheme reminds me of babies and was inspired by the group of solids Bonnie Ouellette sold me at our guild show bazaar in 1999.

When our guild challenged us to make friend-ship exchange quilts, I developed the "Whirling Ribbons" arrangement. "A Moment of My Time" (page 7) reflects the membership of my guild at the time it was made. I also added squares for a few other quilters who are impor-tant to me. I liked the way the resulting geom-etry resembled floating ribbons, so I pieced this pastel version when our daughter announced that a new grandchild was on the way.

When arranging the blocks in this set, I arranged the Rail Fence block in checkerboard fashion, then substituted Nine Patch Variation blocks at certain locations to extend the ribbon tails. You can develop your own geometry in the same fashion, adding as many or as few of the Nine Patch Variation blocks as you wish.

Materials

Yardage based on 42"-wide fabric unless otherwise stated.

⅜ yd. pastel blue solid for blocks and block wedges

¼ yd. *each* pastel green, violet, pink, orange, and yellow solids for blocks and block wedges

⅞ yd. floral print for blocks

1⅜ yds. off-white print for block wedges

¼ yd. *each* medium green, blue, violet, pink, and orange prints for sashing, cornerstones, and binding

⅛ yd. medium yellow print for sashing and corner-stones

1⅜ yds. multicolored print for sashing and binding

2¼ yds. fabric for backing

46" x 62" piece of batting

Cutting

All measurements include ¼"-wide seam allowances.

Use a fine-tip permanent marker to trace the patterns for pieces B–E (pages 78–79) onto a sheet of template plastic. Cut out the templates.

From the pastel blue solid, cut:
- 1 strip, 2" x 42", for Rail Fence and Nine Patch Variation blocks
- 1 strip, 2" x 21", for Rail Fence and Nine Patch Variation blocks
- 4 rectangles, each 2" x 5", for Nine Patch Variation blocks
- 3 strips, each 1¾" x 42", for block wedges

From the pastel green solid, cut:
- 1 strip, 2" x 42", for Rail Fence and Nine Patch Variation blocks
- 1 strip, 2" x 21", for Rail Fence and Nine Patch Variation blocks
- 3 rectangles, each 2" x 5", for Nine Patch Variation blocks
- 2 strips, each 1¾" x 42", for block wedges

From *each* of the pastel violet, pink, and orange solids, cut:
- 1 strip, 2" x 42", for Rail Fence and Nine Patch Variation blocks
- 2 rectangles, each 2" x 5", for Nine Patch Variation blocks
- 2 strips, each 1¾" x 42", for block wedges

From the pastel yellow solid, cut:
- 1 strip, 2" x 35", for Rail Fence and Nine Patch Variation blocks
- 1 rectangle, 2" x 5", for Nine Patch Variation block
- 2 strips, each 1¾" x 42", for block wedges

From the floral print, cut:
- 10 strips, each 2" x 42", for Rail Fence and Nine Patch Variation blocks
- 2 strips, each 2" x 35", for Rail Fence and Nine Patch Variation blocks
- 4 strips, each 2" x 21", for Rail Fence and Nine Patch Variation blocks

From the off-white print, cut:
- 26 strips, each 1¾" x 42", for block wedges

From the medium green print, cut:
- 2 strips, each 1⅞" x 42", for sashing
- 4 squares, each 1⅜" x 1⅜", for cornerstones
- 1 piece B for binding
- 1 piece D for binding
- 1 piece E for binding

From the medium blue print, cut:
- 2 strips, each 1⅞" x 42", for sashing
- 9 squares, each 1⅜" x 1⅜", for cornerstones
- 3 piece B for binding
- 1 piece D for binding
- 1 piece E for binding

From the medium violet print, cut:
- 1 strip, 1⅞" x 42", for sashing
- 6 squares, each 1⅜" x 1⅜", for cornerstones
- 3 piece B for binding

From the medium pink print, cut:
- 1 strip, 1⅞" x 42", for sashing
- 7 squares, each 1⅜" x 1⅜", for cornerstones
- 1 piece B for binding
- 1 piece D for binding
- 1 piece E for binding

From the medium orange print, cut:
- 1 strip, 1⅞" x 42", for sashing
- 5 squares, each 1⅜" x 1⅜", for cornerstones
- 2 piece B for binding
- 1 piece D for binding
- 1 piece E for binding

From the medium yellow print, cut:
- 1 strip, 1⅞" x 42", for sashing
- 4 squares, each 1⅜" x 1⅜", for cornerstones

From the multicolored print, cut:
- 16 strips, each 2" x 42", for sashing
- 14 strips, each 2¼" x 12¾", for binding; trim these pieces using Template C

Making the Blocks

1. Refer to step 2 of Method One for "Rail Fence Blocks" on page 10. Use 1 each of the pastel blue, green, violet, pink, and orange solid 2" x 42" strips and 10 floral 2" x 42" strips to make a total of 5 Rail Fence strip sets, each measuring 5" x 42". Use a pastel strip as the middle (signature) strip in each strip set. Press seams toward the floral strips.

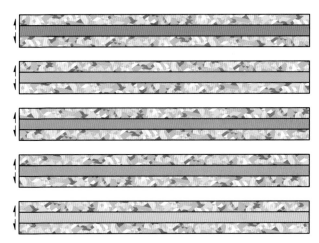

Make 1 each (pastel blue, green, violet, pink, and orange).

2. In a similar fashion, use 1 pastel yellow solid 2" x 35" strip and 2 floral 2" x 35" strips; 1 pastel green solid 2" x 21" strip and 2 floral 2" x 21" strips; and 1 pastel blue solid 2" x 21" strip and 2 floral 2" x 21" strips to make 3 additional Rail Fence strip sets.

Make 1 (pastel yellow).

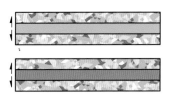

Make 1 each (pastel green and blue).

3. Crosscut a total of 34 segments, each 5" wide, from the strip sets created in steps 1 and 2, in the color combinations indicated in the diagram below. These are the Rail Fence blocks for this quilt. From the remaining strip sets, crosscut 28 segments, each 2" wide, in the colors indicated in the diagram. These will be used to construct the Nine Patch Variation blocks for this quilt.

Make 7
pastel blue.

Make 6
pastel green.

Make 6
pastel violet.

Make 5
pastel pink.

Make 5
pastel orange.

Make 5
pastel yellow.

Make 8
pastel blue.

Make 6
pastel green.

Make 4
pastel violet.

Make 4
pastel pink.

Make 4
pastel orange.

Make 2
pastel yellow.

4. Refer to step 2 of Method One for "Nine Patch Variation Blocks" on page 11. Use the 2" x 5" pastel blue, green, violet, pink, orange, and yellow rectangles and the 28 Nine Patch segments, each 2" wide, from step 3 to make a total of 14 Nine Patch Variation blocks.

Make 4
pastel blue.

Make 3
pastel green.

Make 2
pastel violet.

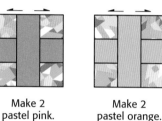

Make 2
pastel pink.

Make 2
pastel orange.

Make 1
pastel yellow.

Adding the Lettering

1. Refer to "Writing on the Blocks" on page 16. If you wish, prepare each block for signature by pressing an appropriately sized strip of freezer paper to the reverse side of the pastel signature area.

2. Refer to "Artistic Lettering" on page 16, and letter the blocks as desired. If you are making a friendship quilt, distribute the blocks for signatures. When the blocks are returned to you, augment the signatures as desired. Heat-set the ink as described on page 19.

Assembling the Quilt Top

1. Use the 13 (total) pastel green, blue, violet, pink, orange, and yellow 1¾" x 42" strips and the 26 off-white 1¾" x 42" strips to make a total of 13 strip sets in the color combinations indicated in the diagram on page 73. Use a pastel strip as the

middle strip in each strip set, and press seams toward the pastel strip. Each strip set should measure 4¼" x 42".

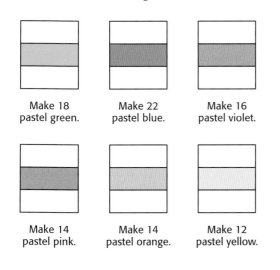

Make 2 each (pastel green, violet, pink, orange, and yellow).

Make 3 pastel blue.

2. Crosscut 96 segments, each 3¹¹⁄₁₆" wide, from the strip sets created in step 1, in the color combinations indicated in the diagram below.

Make 18 pastel green.

Make 22 pastel blue.

Make 16 pastel violet.

Make 14 pastel pink.

Make 14 pastel orange.

Make 12 pastel yellow.

3. Use a ruler and a fine-tip permanent marker to draw a new diagonal line on your cutting mat. Begin the line at the 10" mark along the bottom edge of the mat, and end the line at the 15" horizontal mark on your mat as shown in the diagram below. (If you are working with a large mat,

you can extend this line to the top edge of the mat.) As you draw the new line, you will find that it diagonally crosses 2" x 3" rectangles on the mat.

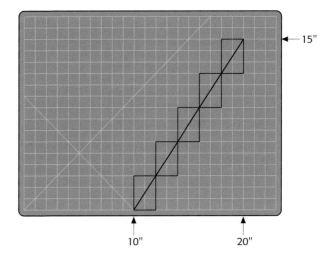

4. Trace pattern A (page 78) onto a sheet of paper. Cut out the paper pattern and tape it to your cutting mat, aligning the diagonal line on the pattern with the diagonal line you drew in step 3. Use your ruler and fine-tip permanent marker to trace the outline of the paper rectangle onto the cutting mat. Remove the tape and the paper.

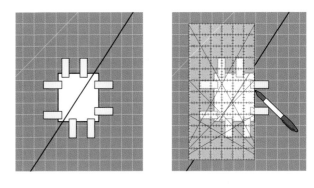

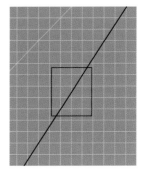

5. Carefully position each segment cut in step 2 over the outline you marked on your cutting mat in step 4. Be sure to orient the pieced segment as shown. Position your ruler over the segment, using the line you drew in step 3 as a guide, and cut each segment on that line. Cut a total of 192 block wedges.

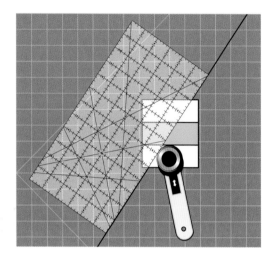

Cut 192 total.

6. Use your design wall or other large, flat surface to arrange the Rail Fence and Nine Patch Variation blocks in 8 horizontal rows of 6 blocks each, orienting them as shown in the assembly diagram on page 76. Surround each block with 4 block wedges, positioning them carefully so that the colors flow as shown. You'll have 4 wedges left over; set these aside for another project.

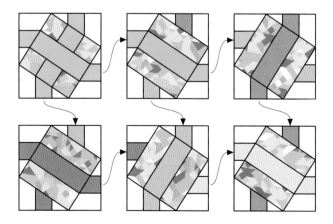

7. Sew 2 of the appropriately colored block wedges to opposite sides of each Rail Fence and Nine Patch Variation block, carefully matching the seams. Press seams toward the wedges. Repeat to sew the remaining 2 triangular wedges to the remaining sides of each block; press. Each block should measure 6¾" x 6¾".

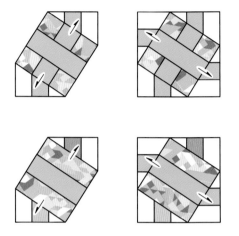

Replace each block in the arrangement after it is sewn, leaving space for the sashing units and the cornerstones.

8. Use the 8 (total) of medium green, blue, violet, pink, orange, and yellow 1⅞" x 42" strips and the 16 multicolored 2" x 42" strips to make a total of 8 strip sets in the color combinations indicated in the diagram below. Use a medium-colored strip as the middle strip in each strip set, and press seams toward the center strip. Each strip set should measure 4⅞" x 42".

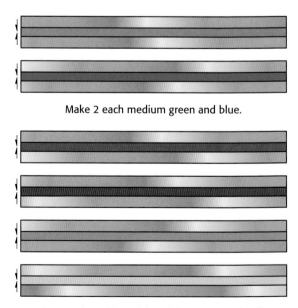

Make 2 each medium green and blue.

Make 1 each medium violet, pink, orange, and yellow.

9. Place each strip set from step 8 on your cutting mat, aligning the long, raw edge of the strip set with the diagonal line you drew in step 3. Use your ruler and rotary cutter to trim off one end of each strip set as shown. To ensure that your ruler is placed correctly, check that the markings on the ruler are parallel to the horizontal and vertical grid marks on the cutting mat.

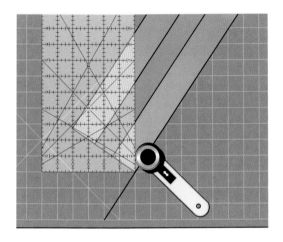

10. Crosscut each strip set along the diagonal edge into segments measuring a scant 1⅜" wide.

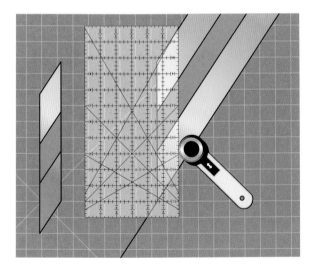

Each strip set should yield approximately 14 segments. Refer to the diagram below to determine how many segments to cut in each color combination.

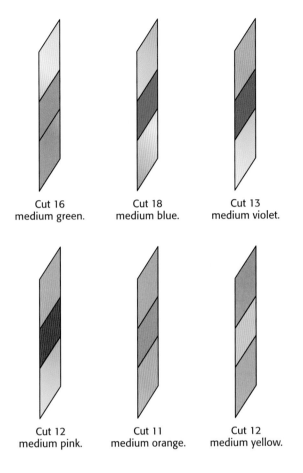

Cut 16
medium green.

Cut 18
medium blue.

Cut 13
medium violet.

Cut 12
medium pink.

Cut 11
medium orange.

Cut 12
medium yellow.

11. Place each segment on the cutting mat and trim off both pointed ends so that each segment measures a scant 1⅜" x 6¾". These segments will be used as the sashing units for your quilt.

12. Refer to the assembly diagram below. Insert 5 vertical sashing units between the 6 blocks in each horizontal row. The medium print in the center of each sashing unit should match the color of the pastel solid in the adjoining blocks.

13. Sew the blocks and sashing units together to make rows 1, 3, 5, 7, 9, 11, 13, and 15. Press seams toward the sashing units.

14. Referring to the assembly diagram, lay out 5 medium print 1⅜" squares and 6 remaining sashing units to form a row between each of the rows assembled in step 13, taking care with the color placement.

15. Sew the medium print squares and sashing units together to make rows 2, 4, 6, 8, 10, 12, and 14. Press seams toward the sashing units.

16. With long raw edges aligned and right sides together, pin the rows together carefully, matching the seams; stitch. Press as desired.

Finishing

Refer to "Finishing Your Project" on pages 26–29 for guidance as needed.

1. Select a quilting design and mark the quilt top as necessary.

2. Divide the backing fabric crosswise into 2 equal panels of approximately 63" each. Remove the selvages and join the panels to make a single, large backing panel.

3. Center the quilt top and batting over the backing. The backing seam should run parallel to the side edges of the quilt top. Pin or thread-baste.

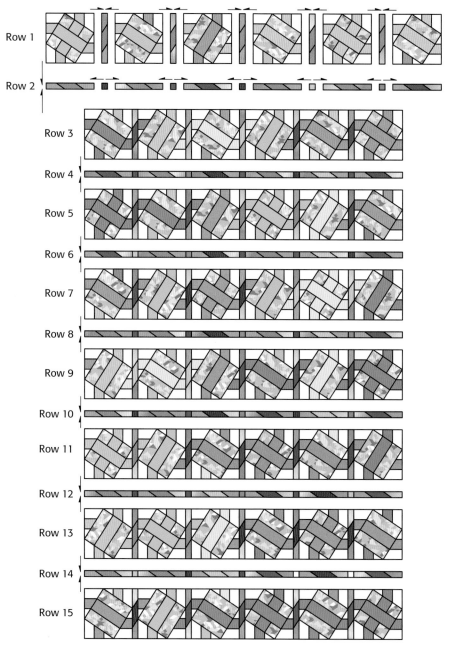

Row 1
Row 2
Row 3
Row 4
Row 5
Row 6
Row 7
Row 8
Row 9
Row 10
Row 11
Row 12
Row 13
Row 14
Row 15

Assembly Diagram

4. Hand or machine quilt as desired.

5. Trim the excess batting and backing so that it is ⅝" past the edge of the quilt top.

6. Arrange the binding pieces (B–E) to make 4 binding strips as shown in the diagram below. Refer to the quilt photo on page 69 for additional guidance, and check the strips against the quilt to make certain that the medium prints in the binding match the pastel solids in the adjoining blocks. Sew pieces B–E together to make the 4 binding strips.

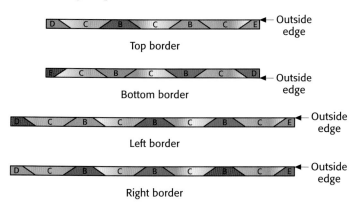

7. Turn under and baste a ¼"-wide hem on the outside edge of each binding strip.

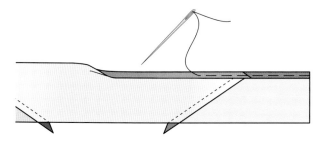

8. With right sides together and long raw edges aligned, and pinning carefully to match seams and colors, sew the left and right binding strips to the appropriate sides of the quilt. Press seams

toward the binding strips. Repeat to sew the top and bottom binding strips to the quilt; press.

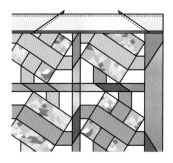

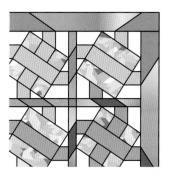

9. Turn each strip to the back of the quilt to create a ⅞"-wide binding, folding and mitering the corners as shown. Blindstitch the binding in place.

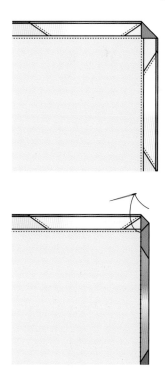

10. Make a label and attach it to your quilt.

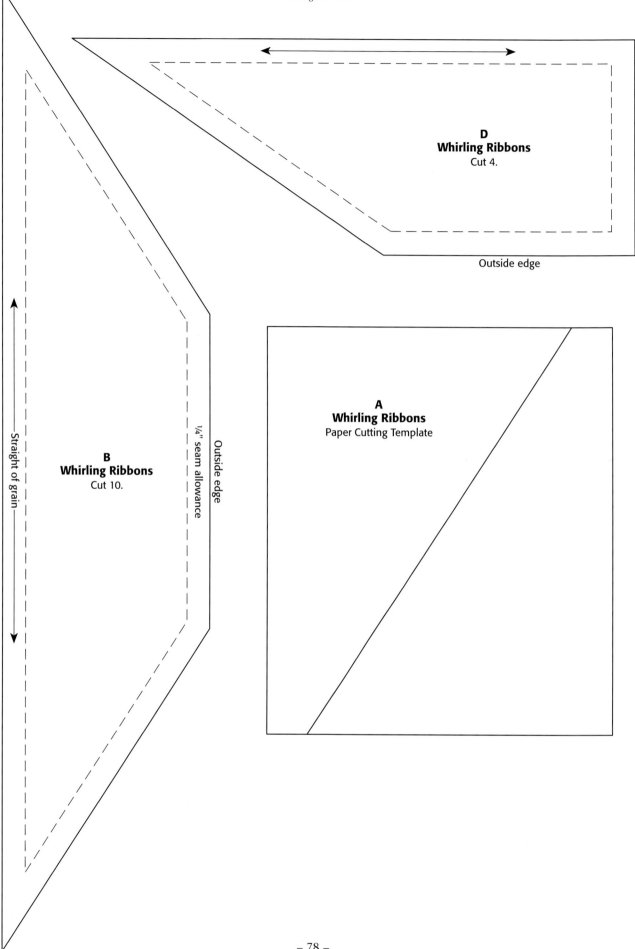

D
Whirling Ribbons
Cut 4.

Outside edge

A
Whirling Ribbons
Paper Cutting Template

Straight of grain

¼" seam allowance

Outside edge

B
Whirling Ribbons
Cut 10.

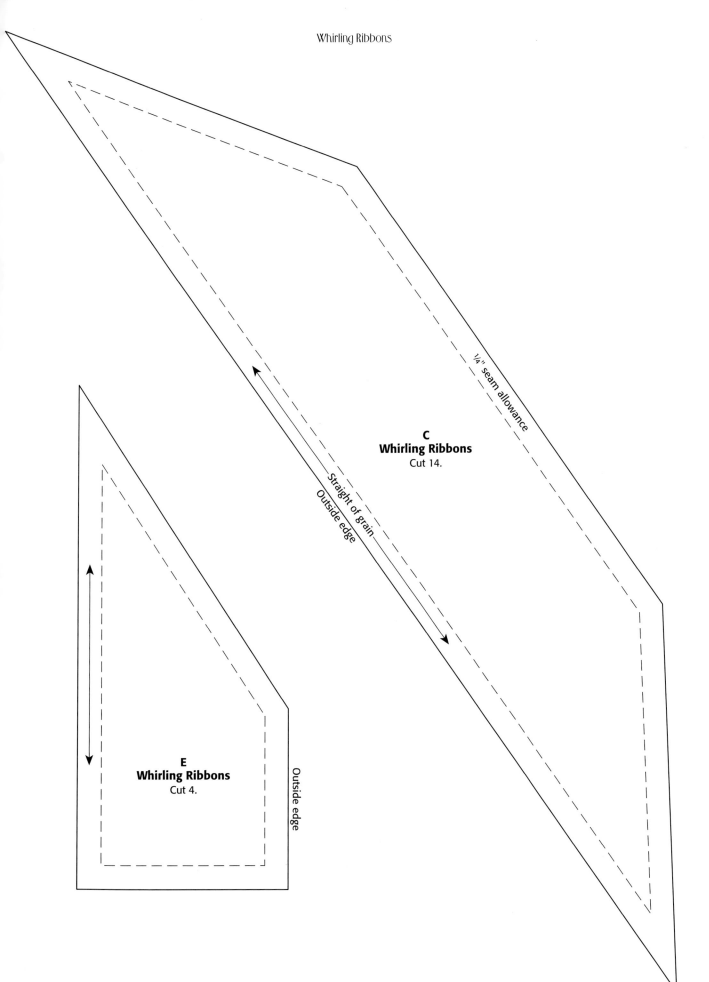

¼" seam allowance

C
Whirling Ribbons
Cut 14.

Straight of grain

Outside edge

E
Whirling Ribbons
Cut 4.

Outside edge

About the Author

When she went to college, Marge Edie didn't know whether to major in art or in math. She chose art and earned a bachelor's degree in fine arts from Ohio University in 1965, where she met and married her husband, Dan. He's a professor of Chemical Engineering at Clemson University in South Carolina, where they've lived for more than twenty-five years. Their son and daughter are both married, and now Marge and Dan are enjoying three sweet grandchildren.

After teaching art in elementary schools for a few years, Marge went back to college for further education in graphic arts and, later, in computer science. New careers as a cameraman in a printing company and then as a senior systems analyst with computer services at Clemson University prepared her for her new life as quilt designer, teacher, and author. Marge's geometric designs are inspired by an interest in math and her experiments on the computer. She explores pattern concepts by working in series.

Marge has written two books on Bargello quilting: *Bargello Quilts* (1994) and *A New Slant on Bargello Quilts* (1998), both published by That Patchwork Place. She also creates arabesque designs, reflecting traditional Hawaiian quilt structures, Moorish architecture, and her interest in symmetry. Marge has taught throughout the country and has exhibited quilts internationally.